SOUND OF HEAVEN

Sound of Heaven

A Treasury of Catholic Verse

edited by
Russell Sparkes

Thomas Raftery CSsp.

ST PAULS

ST PAULS Publishing
187 Battersea Bridge Road, London SW11 3AS, UK
www.stpauls.ie

ISBN 085439 623 3

Set by Tukan DTP, Fareham, UK
Printed by Interprint Ltd., Marsa, Malta

ST PAULS is an activity of the priests and brothers of
the Society of St Paul who proclaim the Gospel
through the media of social communication

A good man was there of religion,
And was a poor parson of a town,
But rich he was of holy thought and work.
He was also a learned man, a clerk,
That Christ's Gospel truly would he preach;
His parishens devoutly would he teach.

(Chaucer)

CONTENTS

ACKNOWLEDGEMENTS

Every effort has been made to trace the owners of the copyright material in this book. It is the Editor's belief that the necessary permissions from publishers, authors, and authorised agents have been obtained. In the case of any question arising as to the use of any material, the Editor will be pleased to make the necessary corrections in future editions of the book.

The Editor gratefully acknowledges permission to reprint copyright material as follows:

'Courtesy'; 'The Prophet lost in the Hills at Evening', and 'The Birds' by Hilaire Belloc © from *The Complete Verse of Hilaire Belloc* are reprinted by permission of PFD on behalf of: The Estate of Hilaire Belloc.

The John Bradburne Memorial Society for permission to reproduce: 'Spring is in the Air', 'Overflow', and 'For a Peal of Eight', by John Bradburne, published in *Songs of the Vagabond* by John Bradburne, © The John Bradburne Memorial Society.

To Jonathan Ball Publishers (Pty) for permission to reproduce the following poems from *Collected Works* Vols I-IV, by Roy Campbell, © originally published by Ad Donker Publishers, Johannesburg, South Africa: 'The Mocking Bird'; 'Mass at Dawn'; 'Christ in the Hospital', including translations from St John of the Cross – 'About the Soul which Suffers with Impatience to See God'; 'With a Divine Intention by the Same Author'; 'Concerning the Divine Word', and 'Summary of Perfection'.

A.P. Watt Ltd on behalf of the Royal Literary Fund for permission to reproduce 'The Donkey' and 'The Convert' by G.K. Chesterton, © from *Poems For All Purposes: the Selected Poems of G.K. Chesterton*, Pimlico 1994.

INTRODUCTION

Religious poetry and its purpose

We struggle to express our deepest feelings and most profound insights. Even when we have the time to sit down with pen and paper, the essence of our ideas somehow seems to escape our best efforts to capture them in prose. Poetry, being based upon regular structures of stress (metre) or sound (rhyme), has the effect of intensifying the idea or experience expressed within it. Many poets use a wide range of images to evoke thought and sensation in the reader's mind. Throughout history, men and women have found that the use of poetry's broad imagery can suggest things otherwise inexpressible in purely logical, linear prose.

Poetry, perhaps more than any other medium, can communicate deep emotion such as the grief felt at the loss of a loved one, or the joy of new love. It can enable us to share with a poet such as Wordsworth the awe that men and women have felt at the sight of great beauty, whether natural or man-made. Religious experience seems akin to the shock of beauty in its ability to transport the readers out of themselves and turn the mind towards the existence of 'permanent things'. Religious verse enables us to hear the greatest minds of the past speaking intimately about these permanent things to us. Cardinal Newman, himself a poet, chose as his personal motto: '*cor ad cor loquitur*' – one heart speaking intimately to another.

In fact a great religious poem is a thing of beauty in its own right, the mind and the inner ear stimulated by the rhythm, sound echoes, and imagery. For example listen to the sound-music of Southwell's 'Mary Magdalen's Lament at Christ's Death' (p.103) or Thompson's 'The Hound of Heaven' (p.217). Like love or music, it has the power to make people happy. However, we should not worry if we find the beauty of poetry uplifting. Ever since the late nineteenth century artists have increasingly sneered at beauty, but as the distinguished theologian Hans Urs von Balthasar wrote in his 1982 book *The Glory of the Lord*:

> Our situation today shows that beauty demands for itself at least as much courage and decision as do truth and goodness, and she will not allow herself to be separated and banned from her two sisters without taking them along in an act of mysterious vengeance. We can be sure that whoever sneers at her name as if she were the ornament of a bourgeois past – whether he admits it or not – can no longer pray and soon will no longer be able to love.

Poetry also has a *reflective* function; its rhythms and repetitions force us to read poetry in a certain way. (I would advise readers new to poetry not to read it silently. Poetry is fundamentally an oral medium that can be best appreciated by being read out loud, or mouthed silently by the reader. This enables the inner ear to 'hear' the poem, the imagination to 'see', the imagery, before the conscious mind works out its apparent meaning.) This reflective and meditative faculty is particularly useful when we approach the mystery that lies at the heart of religion. There is an old saying that: ' a picture is worth a thousand words'. Just as a Rembrandt painting may give us a better insight into the life of Jesus of Nazareth than the dense prose of theology, so too with poetry. Thomas Carlyle once wrote that: 'The poet, like the prophet, is one who has penetrated further into life's mysteries than ordinary men.'

Poetry's origins probably lie in the bards of illiterate society who memorised and thus kept alive the traditions and faith of a people, and it is closely akin to song and religious chant. Think of Homer, Beowulf or the Psalms. Its structures, sounds, repetitions and rhymes may act like a phrase or vision used in meditation as an aid to still our conscious minds. The very act of slowing the mind may help it focus on things of ultimate value. All too often we seem like ships tossed by the waves, our minds restless and rootless in an age driven by the relentless activity of machines. Francis Thompson put this another way in his poem, 'In No Strange Land' (p.216). The author sees Jacob's Ladder rooted in Charing Cross, one of the busiest roads in London. The poem has added poignancy when we learn that Thompson, an alcoholic and drug addict, spent several years sleeping rough on the Embankment Gardens that back on to Charing Cross.

Indeed, we might say that there is a certain similarity between the mystic and the poet, in that both attempt to convey something beyond our normal experience. One critic described poetry as 'penetrative sympathy', in that it can tell us things we did not previously know, but which we then feel we have always known. In Keats' words: 'poetry should strike the reader as a wording of his own highest thoughts, and appear almost as a remembrance'. Keats' description seems particularly true, perhaps, of religious verse. Let me illustrate the point with a simple little anonymous poem, written around 1350, 'I Sing of a Maiden'. (I have put it into modern English.)

I sing of a maiden
Who no man did know;
The King of all kings
As her son she chose.

He came all so still
Where his mother was,
As dew in April
that falleth on the grass.

He came all so still
To his mother's bower,
As dew in April
That falleth on the flower.

He came all so still,
Where his mother lay
As dew in April
That falleth on the spray.

Mother and maiden
Was never such but she
Well may such a lady
God's mother truly be.

This is obviously a meditation on the Incarnation. Yet instead
of theological discourse, the scene is presented to us in a series
of simple images. The language is straightforward, and the
structure of the poem ballad-like in its regular repetition. Yet
it makes us think about the wonder of the Incarnation in
terms we can all understand, of dew falling quietly in April
upon flowers and grass and a spray of leaves. This bypassing
of conceptual thinking to reach a deeper, more intuitive
understanding is a good example of the link between poetry
and mystical thought.

The tradition of Catholic verse

Matthew Arnold once wrote that 'the poet is the best
interpreter of his age'. Having read thousands of poems while
preparing this book, I am inclined to agree with him. This
anthology is therefore built around significant selections from
the major poets of a particular period, such as Robert Southwell

during the Reformation, or Francis Thompson and Alice Meynell during the late Victorian period. There are only brief selections from other poets, designed to give readers a taste of their work. The poems are essentially published in chronological order, using each poet's birth date as a base. (I have put Hopkins outside this sequence, as his poetry was not published until 1918, years after his death. Stylistically it also seems appropriate to class him among the moderns, rather than the Victorians. Similar considerations apply to Tabb.)

What surprised me most in the preparation of this book was the discovery that there has been no explicitly Catholic anthology of religious verse produced in the UK since Frank Sheed's in the 1940s. This raises the question whether there is a distinctly Catholic type of poetry. I think the answer lies in the affirmative. For example, Milton, Bunyan and Herbert are great poets from whom we can learn much, but they write within a Protestant viewpoint of the isolated individual throwing himself upon God's mercy. (Herbert's poem 'The Pulley' is a good example.)

In contrast, Catholicism has always stressed the *person*, defined in relation to other men, rather than the *individual*, defined as distinct from other men. It is only natural that a distinctly Catholic theology and insight into religious practice should find expression in verse. I therefore feel that it is quite reasonable to say that there is a distinct corpus of poetry, written by Catholics, and on explicitly Catholic themes, which we may call 'Catholic poetry'. (We live in querulous and pluralistic times. Older Catholic writers would have regarded it as self-evident that there must be Catholic poetry, arguing that the practice of the Faith affects all we think and do, including the writing of verse.)

Let us think, for example, of *sacramental awareness*, often poetically expressed as simple rejoicing in the quiet communal practice of the Faith. Think of the mediæval poem '*Deo Gracias*' (p.62) as well as Chaucer's 'Poor Parson' (p.71), or Alice Meynell's 'General Communion' (p.208). Perhaps my favourite exposition of this theme is the wonderful poem,

'Low Mass on Sunday' (p.281) by Caryll Houselander, herself
a mystic. 'Low Mass on Sunday' notes the all too human
failings of priest and congregation, but proclaims with quiet
intensity the spiritual reality underlying it all. It begins:

> The church is noisy with shuffle of children's feet,
> and somebody's endless cough.
> The heads of the boys in rows
> are knobs of unpolished wood,
> mahogany, teak, and pine.

Another characteristic theme of Catholic verse is the
expression of joy and awe at the Incarnation. The mystery of
the mother of God is something frequently treated by
Catholic poets, as well as her heartbreak at the foot of the
Cross. Devotion to Our Lady was of course present across
Christendom in the Middle Ages, but it was so intense in
England that the country was given the title of 'Our Lady's
Dower'. (While 'dower' can mean dowry, it has a more
general meaning than marriage portion, i.e. as a special gift
set aside for some purpose.)

I mentioned earlier that both love and religious passion
are two of the main well-springs of verse writing. In fact, the
saints resemble lovers in that they often feel their experiences
welling up within them and bursting forth in song or verse.
This has been true since the birth of Christianity – and this
feeling is beautifully expressed in the psalms. This sense of
awe, joy, and love was perhaps particularly characteristic of St
Francis of Assisi, and I am pleased to be able to include in this
volume translations, by distinguished English poets, of two of
his best poems, 'The Canticle of the Sun', and 'Set Love in
Order' (pp. 47,48). Many of Francis' songs are pure hymns of
praise to God, and his whole life can be seen as an act of
adoration. When Cardinal Hume knew that he was dying, he
wrote to a fellow monk saying how pleased he was. This
ability to welcome death, let alone to accept it, is surely a
distinguishing mark of great personal spirituality. St Francis

expressed it with typical vigour by thanking God for 'Sister Death'. Yet the broader wonder at existence is a distinctive characteristic of Christian thinking that is naturally expressed in verse. In the words of the Victorian poet Coventry Patmore:

What is gladness without gratitude,
And where is gratitude without God?

I have used three main criteria when examining poems for inclusion in this anthology: they should be of clear literary merit; on Catholic themes, and by Catholic authors. As a general rule I have decided only to include poems by poets who were either born or received into the Catholic Church, and who practised their faith for a period of time. This excludes poets like Marvell and Blanco-White who briefly joined the Church, but then apostatised, as well as death-bed converts like Oscar Wilde.

William Shakespeare grew up within a devoutly Catholic family, and there is significant, though not conclusive, evidence that he remained a Catholic sympathiser all his life. We should note that his verse was written for public consumption at a time when it would have been dangerous to openly proclaim Catholic allegiance; given that background, his Catholic sympathies seem unmistakable. Take, for example, Shakespeare's positive depiction of the Friar in *Romeo and Juliet* (p.118), or in *Measure for Measure* written at a time when friars were generally portrayed as sexually licentious rogues. The line in Sonnet 73, 'Bare ruined choirs, where once the sweet birds sang', is often taken to refer to the despoilation of the monasteries. The doctrine of Purgatory and prayers for the dead were traditional Catholic practices most fiercely attacked by the Protestant Reformers. Yet Henry V, Shakespeare's model of an ideal king, sets up chantries to pray for the soul of the murdered Richard II. The Ghost in *Hamlet* (p.116) proclaims a staunchly Catholic view. His tortured account of his death ends: 'unhousled, unannealed' (no Last Rites, no Blessed Sacrament), 'O horror! O horror! Most horror!'

I have made a few exceptions to the above rule. It seems reasonable to include translations of Catholic poetry by non-Catholics. I have also included three poets whose work seems to me to be intrinsically Catholic: R.S. Hawker, as well as Christina and Dante Gabriel Rossetti. Hawker was a Church of England priest who was received into the Catholic Church on his deathbed. Christina Rossetti's poetry in particular is of a distinctly Catholic nature. Her life and work indicates a vocation to be a nun. Both her parents came from devoutly Catholic families, but her father lapsed and poisoned her mind against Rome by the most virulent anti-clericalism. After he had a nervous breakdown, both Christina and her mother took refuge in high Anglo-Catholicism, but she was never able to come to terms with Rome. Her brother Dante Gabriel Rossetti called for a priest on his deathbed, but died before the latter arrived. (The last poem in the book is by the non-Catholic Henry Adams, as will be explained later.)

English Christendom – the Dower of Our Lady

There are two other themes that I wish to highlight in this introduction. The first is the period of over nine hundred years when England was an integral part of western Christendom, from St Augustine's mission to the Anglo-Saxons in 596 until the Reformation broke up the mediæval unity of Christendom. Religious devotion was the basis and the bedrock of this civilisation.

Indeed, the oldest known work in the English language is a hymn of praise. Caedmon was a humble and illiterate shepherd, rough-voiced and too shy to join in the Latin worship of the Northumbrian monastery where he worked. One night in a dream an angel visited him and told him to get up and sing. To the astonishment of all the monks, he did so in a beautiful voice. Caedmon's hymn (p.38) is dated to about the year 675. There is little doubt about the authenticity of the poem, which survives in a variety of sources in an early Northumbrian dialect. The story of Caedmon's dream was written down a few years after it happened by Bede who lived nearby, and who may have based his account on monks who knew Caedmon personally. Some two hundred years later an unknown Anglo-Saxon author gave us one of the greatest religious poems in the English language, 'The Dream of the Rood' (rood = cross). Of course, Old English is a foreign tongue to us now, and all three Anglo-Saxon poems have therefore been included in modern translation.

But if Old English is totally incomprehensible to us now, the same is true of Middle English (roughly 1100-1450). Much great religious poetry was written during this period, as only to be expected from a period when people's lives were dominated and based upon religion. I had hoped to be able to include some examples with the help of footnotes, but after due thought decided that this simply wouldn't work. I came to the conclusion that the ordinary reader would be put off by Middle English owing to its obsolete vocabulary and strange spelling. I felt that he/she would ignore mediæval poetry and proceed to poems that are recognisably modern English.

It seemed a shame to leave out religious verse written when life in England was founded upon spiritual ideals, and a great loss of our cultural heritage. I therefore decided to translate some of the best of them myself. I hope that these versions will give modern readers a taste of the profound poetry written when Catholic England was an integral part of Christian Europe. I certainly make no claims that my translations are great poetry, but my aims will have been achieved if they enable the general reader to see the bones of the great poetry that lies beneath them. (My excuse for translating them is that I am unaware of anybody else having done so in verse form, and that they are otherwise inaccessible to the modern reader.)

The one exception I have made is Chaucer, whose verse is much more accessible than that of his contemporaries such as Langland. (It also seemed wrong to translate the 'father of English poetry'.) I therefore hope that I have made Chaucer reasonably intelligible to the general reader by modernising the spelling with an occasional footnote provided for obsolete words, as has been my practice for poems by early Tudors such as Skelton and Thomas More.

Modern man seems fixated by the sense of the new and the lure of the modern. It is almost as if he is frightened of time, ignorant of history, and terrified of death – the last taboo. Mediæval man thought of death all the time – and of what lay after. Look at 'Where Are They Now?' (p.48) where the poet notes the arrogance and swagger of the rich and powerful – and their eventual fate, or 'Wait a While', a short poem about 'postponing' God's call. I find these reminders of death's proximity striking, coming from people who died almost a thousand years ago. In the wake of the Black Death, around 1350, the late Middle Ages had a particular preoccupation with death, for example John Audelay's (c1360-1430) poem '*Timor mortis conturbat me – passio Christi conforta me*' (p.74) (the fear of death confounds me – the passion of Christ consoles me). (There is also a poem on the same theme by William Dunbar.)

Perhaps the particular genius of the Middle Ages was best expressed in meditation upon the passion of Our Lord, such as 'The Dream of the Rood'. Some of the poems on this theme are of great poignancy, for example the dialogue between Our Lord on the Cross and Our Lady in 'There Stood a Mother' (p.44), or '*Stabat Mater*', an alternate vision of Our Lady at the foot of the Cross. There are hymns of praise to Mary, and frequent invocations for her help, as in the 'Prisoner's Song' (p.43).

Priests as Poets

Catholic verse has one unique and important feature that is rarely mentioned – the great contribution that priests and other religious have made to the treasury of Catholic verse we have inherited. English literature owes a debt to the Society of Jesus for having given us two of the greatest poets in the language in Robert Southwell, priest and martyr, and Gerard Manley Hopkins. Hopkins belongs to that small number of poets who have transformed the way we think about poetry.

Take, for instance, a few lines from 'God's Grandeur':

> The world is charged with the grandeur of God.
> It will flame out, like shining from shook foil;
> It gathers to a greatness, like the ooze of oil
> Crushed. Why do men then now not reck his rod?

The first line is fairly conventional, a tetrameter in mostly iambic form. The metre then becomes less regular, while the striking second line combines an illuminating image (the grandeur of God is like light reflected in a thousand ways from shaken foil) with a crushing dissonance, i.e. the ugly clash of the letter 'k' at the end of 'shook' with the following letter 'f', an ugliness compounded by the sound echoes of the long vowels 'oo' and 'oi'. Yet Hopkins had such a wonderful poetic ear that it seems practically certain that this dissonance is intentional, presumably intended to make us reflect more intensely upon the line.

Hopkins and Southwell are, however, relatively well known. It may be briefly worth mentioning some of the other religious who have contributed to this great tradition. Caedmon was mentioned earlier. Bede himself, priest and monk at Jarrow, and the father of English history, composed a celebrated 'Death Song' on his deathbed. Mediæval England produced a number of great mystics, such as Julian of Norwich, Margaret Kempe, Walter Hilton, as well as the unknown author of *The Cloud of Unknowing*. One of them, Richard Rolle (1290-1349), was also a poet, as well as being a hermit and spiritual adviser to a community of nuns. His poem 'A Song of the Passion' (p.60) is clearly a meditation on Our Lord's passion, and may well have been written for pastoral use, as we know that religious poetry was widely used in homilies during the period.

Other mediæval priestly poets included John Lydgate and John Skelton. The latter wrote some spiritual verse in his characteristic terse style while acting in old age as Henry VIII's tutor. The Franciscan novice William Dunbar was one of the fathers of Scottish dialect poetry. One of the greatest mystics of the Catholic Church was St John of the Cross, who experienced the rapture and terror of what he called the 'dark night of the soul', which he expressed in verse. He is regarded as one of the greatest poets in Spanish, and English readers are fortunate that his poems have been translated into English by Roy Campbell, a highly talented poet in his own right (p.285).

The Reformation gave us martyr poets like the Jesuits Henry Walpole (1555-1595) and John Thewlis (1580-1616). It was said of Walpole that his hands had been so broken by torture that he had to hold a pencil in both hands in order to write, yet his poems (many of them written in captivity) express great joy. But the greatest of them all as a poet was surely Robert Southwell. Here are a few lines from 'Mary Magdalen's Lament at Christ's Death':

Sith my life from life is parted:
Death come take thy portion,
Who survives, when life is murdered,
Lives by mere extortion.
All that live, and not in God,
Couch their life in death's abode.

Seely stars must needs leave shining,
When the sun is shadowed
Borrowed streams refrain their running,
When head springs are hindered.
One that lives by others' breath,
Dyeth also by his death.

When reading Southwell it should be remembered that his poetry was either written when 'on the run' from Walsingham's priest hunters, or in the Tower after suffering excruciating torture. Its quality given this provenance is astonishing. Catholic priests during this period faced the horrors of the death penalty for high treason: hanging, drawing, and quartering. Hanging as a form of public execution in the twentieth century was designed to break the neck and bring quick death, but in this period it was a form of slow strangulation. The victim was cut down shortly before death, revived, and then 'drawn' by having his entrails pulled out. During Southwell's execution his bearing so enthused the crowd that they refused to let the hangman cut him down until his death was certain. Southwell's poems were published in book form shortly after his martyrdom in 1595 under the title of *St Peter's Complaint*, and were so popular that the book ran into several editions.

The only priestly poet of note in the following century was Richard Crashaw (1612-1649), who ended his days at the Cathedral of Loretto. I find Crashaw's more baroque style to be rather off-putting at times, but there is undeniable power in his 'Hymn to St Teresa' and the simpler 'Spiritual Epigrams'. Crashaw was followed by a long silence, as there was in Catholic poetry generally following the death of Dryden and Pope, until the Catholic revival in the middle of the nineteenth century. Cardinal Newman (1801-1890) played a notable part in this revival as he did in so many other areas of Catholic life. As well as the great epic *The Dream of Gerontius* Newman gave us many popular hymns, as did his fellow priest Frederick Faber (1814-1863). At the end of the nineteenth century a number of poets such as Lionel Johnson and Ernest Dowson recoiled from Wilde's aesthetic movement by becoming Catholics. John Gray (1866-1934), the inspiration for Wilde's book *The Portrait of Dorian Gray*, took this one step further by becoming a parish priest in Edinburgh.

Also worthy of note are the American priest John Bannister Tabb (1845-1909) with his concentrated, pithy verse, and Mgr R.H. Benson (1870-1914), who was the son of a celebrated Archbishop of Canterbury but became a well-known Catholic apologist. The twentieth century has given us few significant priestly poets, though I would mention Fr Leo Ward (1896-1942), a descendent of 'Ideal' Ward, who died of ill treatment in a Japanese prisoner-of-war camp. American religious such as Sr Maris Stella and Fr John Lynch also played a major part in the flowering of Catholic literature in US during the early twentieth century. Lay people who were attracted to the religious life and who wrote poetry included David Jones (1895-1974), Caryll Houselander (1901-1954) and the hermit John Bradburne (1921-1979).

Poetry for the modern world

Poetry is not just for our individual gratification and edification. It is an essential part of the culture that we have inherited from our ancestors. Western civilisation was built upon the congruence of Greek inquiry and the moral and spiritual foundation provided by Christianity. For almost a thousand years in England that meant Catholic Christianity, and the poetry written before and during the Reformation can help us understand the history that lies behind and beneath us.

The twentieth century has had the arrogance to reject this tradition, but the result of the abandonment of traditional Christian morality has not been the worldly happiness sought by its proponents. Twentieth-century art and literature has been dominated by gloom about life, calling it pointless, meaningless, vacant. The author or artist feels him- or herself alone and in despair. I hope that the poetry published in this book illustrates this older wisdom, and perhaps it may reassure the reader who feels at odds with the modern world that the problem lies with modern society itself. The great Roman Empire was curiously modern in its military might, material wealth, and worship of sensuality. But it eventually collapsed, and the knowledge of civilisation itself would have been lost had it not been for the monks who kept it alive during the six centuries of the Dark Ages. It is arguable that we have now entered a new Dark Age, at least in terms of moral values; perhaps the Catholic Church is, once again, keeping alive knowledge, truth and wisdom for future generations.

The twentieth century was not a great period for religious

verse; indeed relatively little of high quality was written at this time. Nevertheless, one of the things I am most proud of in preparing this anthology is having rediscovered three major twentieth-century Catholic poets: Roy Campbell (particularly his translations of St John of the Cross); Michael Ffinch and Caryll Houselander. All three are highly accomplished from a technical point of view, and all three have their own distinctive poetic voice and vision. Their work is generally ignored in secular anthologies of twentieth-century verse. I suspect that this is probably due more to their vision of 'permanent things' being unpalatable to the modern literary establishment, rather than to any literary deficiency. If inclusion here helps awaken interest in their work I shall feel well rewarded for my work as editor.

The last poem in this book is a meditation by one of America's greatest and most civilised scholars, Henry Adams. In his 'Prayer to the Virgin of Chartres' (p.306) he looks back with longing from the empty efficiency and meretricious bustle of modern life to the still certainties of the thirteenth century. Adams' unfulfilled longing lends a touch of personal intensity to the general questing of the poem. In the Middle Ages it was customary to end a verse form such as a ballad with an *envoi*, or brief conclusion. Let the 'Prayer to the Virgin of Chartres' be the *envoi* of this book.

Russell Sparkes, Christmas 2000

PART I

English Christendom
596-1535

It is easy to forget that for over 900 years England was an integral part of Christian Europe, or Christendom. Men had seen a great empire collapse despite enormous riches and military might. Yet despite its power, the Roman Empire proved to have feet of clay in its moral foundations – its worship of sex and materialism. Christendom was an attempt to rebuild civilisation from the wreck of Rome based upon Gospel values. Every aspect of life was imbued with Christian ideals, and this is reflected in the poetry written at the time – much of it anonymous.

Caedmon c630-675 (translated by Russell Sparkes)

Hymn

Now let us praise Heaven's Kingdom keeper,
God of power, the thought behind all,
Father of glory and works of wonder,
From the beginning Eternal Lord and God.
First, the Holy Creator, for the children of men,
Made the roof of heaven.
Then, the Guardian of mankind, eternal Lord,
Filled the earth for Man's good.
Praise Thee, Lord and God Almighty.

Bede c670-735 (translated by Russell Sparkes)

Death Song

Before this forced journey,
That none may escape,
The wise man feels the need
To consider, before
His going hence,
The state of his soul.
Is it pure with good,
Or stained with evil?
On the death-day,
Will it be judged worthy?

Anonymous c900 (translated by Helen Gardner)

The Dream of the Rood [1]

Listen! I will tell the most treasured of dreams,
A dream that I dreamt the deep middle of the night,
After the race of men had gone to their rest.
It seemed to me I saw the strangest of Trees,
Lifted aloft in the air, with light all around it,
Of all Beams the brightest. It stood as a beacon,
Drenched in gold; gleaming gems were set
Fair around its foot; five such flamed

High upon its cross-branch. Hosts of angels gazed on it
In world-without-end glory. This was no felon's gallows.
Holy souls in heaven hailed it with wonder
And mortal men on earth and all the Maker wrought.
Strange was that Tree of Triumph — and I a transgressor,
Stained by my sins. I saw the Tree of Glory
Bright with streaming banners, brilliantly shining,
Gilded all with gold. Glittering jewels
Worthily adorned the Tree of the World's Ruler.
Yet beneath the gold I glimpsed the signs
Of some ancient agony when again, as of old,
Its right side sweated blood. Sorrow seized me;
I was full of fear. I saw the beacon flicker,
Now dazzling, now darkened; at times drenched and
      dripping
Running red with blood, at times a royal treasure.
Yet even so I lay there for a long while,
Sorrowing at the sight of my Saviour's Tree;
When on a sudden I heard it speak;
The precious wood uttered these words:

'Many years ago — the memory abides —
I was felled to the ground at the forest's edge,
Severed from my roots. Enemies seized me,
Made of me a mark of scorn for criminals to mount on;
Shoulder — high they carried me and set me on a hill.
Many foes made me fast there. Far off then I saw
The King of all mankind coming in great haste,
With courage keen, eager to climb me.
I did not dare, against my Lord's dictate,
To bow down or break, though I beheld tremble
The earth's four corners. I could easily
Have felled his foes; yet fixed and firm I stood.
Then the young Hero — it was God Almighty —
Strong and steadfast, stripped himself for battle;
He climbed up on the high gallows, constant in his purpose,
Mounted it in sight of many, mankind to ransom.

Horror seized me when the Hero clasped me,
But I dared not bow or bend down to earth,
Nor falter, nor fall; firm I needs must stand.
I was raised up a Rood, a royal King I bore,
The High King of Heaven: hold firm I must.
They drove dark nails through me, the dire wounds
    still show,
Cruel gaping gashes, yet I dared not give as good.
They taunted the two of us; I was wet with teeming blood,
Streaming from the warrior's side when he sent forth
    his spirit.
High upon that hill helpless I suffered
Long hours of torment; I saw the Lord of Hosts
Outstretched in agony; all embracing darkness
Covered with thick clouds the corpse of the World's Ruler;
The bright day was darkened by a deep shadow,
All its colours clouded; the whole creation wept,
Keened for its King's fall; Christ was on the Rood.

Yet warriors from afar eagerly came speeding
To where he hung alone. All this I beheld.
Sore sorrow seized me, yet I stooped to men's hands
Humbly, but with courage keen. They clasped
    Almighty God,
Raised him from the rack; me they let remain,
Standing soaked in blood, wounded by sharp arrows.
They laid his wearied limbs on earth; the watchers at
    his head
Looked down on the Lord of Heaven, lying there at rest
Forspent from his great fight. Then they framed for him
    a tomb,
Shaped it of bright stone in the sight of me who slew him.
They laid in it the Lord of Victories, then raised the
    loud lament,
Sang at the sunsetting, then sadly turned away,
Left their glorious Lord. Alone he lay and rested there.
But we three weeping for a long while yet

Stood at our stations as there sank into silence
The cry of the warriors. The corpse grew cold,
The soul's sweet dwelling-place. Us they then struck down,
Felled us all to earth, awful was our fate.
They dug a deep pit, deep down they buried us;
Yet even there the Lord's friends, his faithful thanes
found me.
With gleaming gold and silver they made me glorious.

Now you have heard – beloved hero –
How I endured the evil men did to me,
Suffered great sorrow. Now the season is come
When all things honour me, here and everywhere,
Mortal men on earth and all the Maker wrought;
They bow before this beacon. On me the Only Begotten,
The Son of God suffered; and so in splendour now
I tower high under heaven; and I have power to heal
Each and all who honour me and hold me in awe.
I was deemed in former days the direst of torments,
I was hated and abhorred until I made a highway,
The right Way of Life, for the race of men.
Lo, the King of Glory, the Keeper of the Gates of Heaven,
Favoured me above all the trees of the forest,
Even as his maiden-mother, Mary herself,
Almighty God favoured above all womankind.

Now, therefore, I bid you – beloved hero –
Say what you have seen to the sons of men,
Make manifest in words the mystery of the Beam of Glory
On which Almighty God endured bitter throes,
For all mankind and for their many sins,
And for Adam's deed done ages since.
Death he drank there; yet from death the Lord arose
With might and power to be man's helper.
He ascended into heaven, yet hither again
To this middle world he will come, once more to
seek mankind.

At the Last Day, the Lord himself,
Almighty God, attended by angels,
Will descend to give doom – who has power to give doom –
To each and every man as erewhile here
In this earthly life he earned evil or good.
Nor may any man there be unafraid
When he hears the words the World's Ruler will utter.
He will ask in sight of many where is the man
Who for the Lord's sake would give up life,
Drink bitter death as he did on the Beam;
And all then shall fear and few of them will know
How justly they may answer Christ the Judge of all.
But none need be afraid to abide his appearing
Who has borne in his bosom this brightest of beacons.
For through this Cross shall come to the Kingdom,
From this earthly life, each and every soul
Who longs with his Lord to live in life everlasting.'

Then I prayed to that blessed Beam, blithe in spirit,
With courage keen; no comrade was by me,
I lay there alone. There was longing in my heart,
I was fain to fare forth; and since then I have felt
Many hours of longing. I live my life in hope
That I may trust in and seek that Tree of Triumph,
Alone honour and serve it above all others.
This is my heart's desire; in this is my delight;
My refuge is the Rood. Rich friends and mighty
I have none to help me, for they have gone hence,
Left this world's glories to seek the King of Glory,
They live now in Heaven with the High Father,
They abide in bliss; and here below I wait
For the coming of the day when the Cross of my Lord
Which here on this earth my own eyes have looked on,
From this fleeting life will fetch my soul away
And will bring me then where there is much bliss,
Great gladness in Heaven, where the people of God
Are seated at his Feast in fullness of joy,

And me there will set down where I hereafter may
Abide in bliss and among the blessed
Take my fill of joy. May the Lord be my friend,
Who erstwhile on earth endured bitter throes,
Suffered on the gallows-tree for the sins of men.
He loosed us from bondage and life he gave to us
And a home in Heaven. Hope sprang up again
Bright with blessing to those burning in pain.
Christ the Son of God journeyed as a Conqueror,
Mighty and Victorious, when with many in his train,
A great company of souls, he came to God's Kingdom –
The one Almighty to the bliss of the angels
And of all the holy ones who in heavenly places
Abode in glory – when Almighty God,
The King of Kings, came home to his own country.

1. Rood (Anglo-Saxon 'Rod') means cross – it still survives in the term rood-screen.

Anonymous c1150 (translated by Russell Sparkes)

Prisoner's Song

Once, then, I knew trouble not,
Now I must lament my lot.
Full of care I sigh,
Guiltless I am, but heavy with shame.
O God help! For thy sweet name,
King of heaven on high.

Jesus Christ, true God, true man,
Lord – have pity upon me!
Out of this prison where I am
Bring me out and make me free.
For I and my brothers,
God knows I lie not –
Were for the sins of others
To this foul prison a-brought.

Almighty,
That well lightly,
Gives peace and remedy,
Heaven's King,
From this suffering
Bring us out.
Forgive them,
The wicked men,
If it is thy will
For whose guilt,
We were thrust
Into this prison ill.

Hope not in this life.
Here none may remain.
High though he may rise,
Death cuts him down again.
Now man has wealth and bliss;
But soon he shall feel their loss,
Worldly wealth, for sure,
Lasts but an hour.

Maiden, who bore heaven's King,
Beseech thy son, the sweetest thing,
For his mercy on our plight,
To bring us out of this suffering.
May he bring us from this woe,
And teach us in this life so
To act, whatever life may bring,
That we may ever gain
Thy eternal bliss.

Anonymous c1150 (translated by Russell Sparkes)

Stabat Mater

There Jesus Christ's mother stood,
Beheld her Son on the rood, [1]

That He was tortured on;
The Son hung, the mother stood,
And beheld her child's blood
From His wounds down it ran.

When He died, the King of life,
No woman knew more grief
Than thou did then, Lady.
The bright day turned into night
When Jesus Christ, thy heart's delight,
Was racked with pain and woe.

Thy whole being ached with loss,
When thou saw'st His bloody wounds,
And the corpse down from the Cross.
His wounds sore and smart,
Stung and pierced thy heart,
As Simeon had foretold.

Now His head with blood bedecked,
Now His side with spear pierced,
Thou beheld, O gracious Lady.
Now His hands spread on the rood,
Now His feet awash with blood
And nailed to the tree.

Now His flesh with scourges beaten;
And His blood so widely shaken
Made thy head so sore.
Whereas the crowd tried to hide their eyes,
Thy eyes were fixed on His agony-
No man could suffer more.

Now is the time for thee to yield,
The word that thou from Him withheld
When thy Child was born.
Now He asketh with intent,

What in thy child-bearing,
Was kept from Him before.

Now thou findest, mother mild,[2]
What all women suffer when with child,
Though pure maiden that thou be.
Now to thee are quick, hard and dure,
The pains whereof to thee forbore,
In child-birth to appear.

Soon, after the night of sorrow
Springs up the light of morrow.
In thine heart, sweet maid,
Thy sorrows shall turn to bliss.
For thy son, sure it is,
Rose up on the third day.

But then thou wert so blithe
When He rose from death to life!
Through the stone complete He glid;
Just as in His birth he did.
Both after and before,
Intact remained thy maidenhead.

To new bliss He now is brought
Who mankind so dearly bought
And gave His dear life for us.
Gladness and joy us thou make,
For thy sweet Son's sake,
Blessed maiden, mother joyous.

Queen of heaven, for thy bliss,
Lighten all our sorrowfulness.
Turn our ill into good.
Bring us, mother to thy Son.
Make us live with Him for ever,
Who brought us with His blood.
Amen.

1. Rood = cross.   2. Mild = gentle.

St Francis of Assisi 1181-1226
(translated by Matthew Arnold)

The Canticle of the Sun

O most high, almighty, good Lord God,
To Thee belong praise, glory, honour and all blessing!
Praised be my Lord God with all His creatures,
And especially our brother the sun,
Who brings us the day and who brings us the light;
Fair is he and shines with very great splendour;
O Lord, he signifies to us Thee!
Praised be my Lord for our sister the moon, and for
    the stars,
The which He has set clear and lovely in heaven.
Praised be my Lord for our brother the wind,
And for air and cloud, calms and all weather
By which Thou upholdest life in all creatures.

Praised be my Lord for all those who pardon one another,
For His love's sake, and who endure weakness and
    tribulation;
Blessed are they who peaceably shall endure.
For Thou, O Most Highest, shalt give them a crown!
Praised be my Lord for our sister,
The death of the body, from which no man escapeth.
Woe to him who dieth in mortal sin!
Blessed are they who are found walking
By Thy most holy will, for the second death
Shall have no power to do them harm.
Praise ye and bless the Lord,
And give thanks unto Him and serve Him
With great humility.

St Francis of Assisi 1181-1226
(translated by D.G. Rossetti)

Set Love in Order

Set Love in order, thou that lovest Me,
Never was virtue out of order found;
And though I fill thy heart desirously,
By thine own virtue I must keep My ground;

When to My love thou dost bring charity,
Even she must come with order girt and gowned.
Look how the trees are bound
To order, bearing fruit;
And by one thing compute
In all things earthly, order's grace or gain.

All earthly things I had the making of
Were numbered and were measured then by Me;
And each was ordered to its end by Love,
Each kept, through order, clean for ministry.
Charity most of all, when known enough,
Is of her very nature orderly.
Lo, now! what heat in thee,
Soul, can have bred this rout?
Thou put'st all order out,
Even this love's heat must be its curb and rein.

Anonymous c1200 (translated by Russell Sparkes)

Where Are They Now?

Where are they now who before us were,
Led hounds to hunt, and hawks bore,
Masters of woods and field?
The rich ladies in their bower
Wore gold in their coiffeur,
Their cheeks with powder red.

Eating and drinking was their treasure,
Their life one long feast of pleasure.
Before them all men did kneel,
Their bearing proud and high.
And, in a twinkling of an eye,
Their souls were lost.

Where now the laughter, where now the song,
Where the rich robes and the step so proud,
The joy of hawk and hound?
All that happiness has gone away,
Their wealth turned to lackaday,
To torment and trial are they bound.

They took the path of pleasure here,
And now they lie in hell-fire,
The fire that burns for ever.
Long is aye, long is o,
Long the pain and long the woe,
Out thence come they never.

Stand firm, then, man, if thou canst,
A little torment that thee hurts.
Forbear thy pleasure oft;
Though needle-sharp be thy pain,
Think of what thou standst to gain,
To thee it will seem soft.

If Satan, that foul thing,
Through wicked words, or false tempting,
Should knock thee down,
Get up! And be of good heart
Stand firm, do not fall again,
It lasts but a little while.

Take the Cross to thy staff,
Think of him that on it gave

His life which was so dear.
He gave for thee, thou owes it Him,
Take the staff against his foe,
And beat him as a thief.

Maiden-mother, heaven's queen,
Thou may and can and ought to be,
Our shield against the fiend.
Help us to shun all sin,
That we may see thy Son,
In joy without end.

Anonymous c1200 (translated by Russell Sparkes)

Of One that is so Fair and Bright

Of one that is so fair and bright
Velut maris stella [1]
Brighter than the day's light
Parens et puella [2]
I cry to thee; look down on me!
Lady, pray to thy Son for me,
Tam pia, [3]
That I may come to thee,
Maria.
Lady, flower of every thing,
Rosa sine spina, [4]
Thou bore Jesu, Heaven's King,
Gratia divina. [5]
Of all that beyond all price
Lady, Queen of Paradise
Electa; [6]
Maiden, mother mild, in this
Effecta. [7]

All this world was forlorn
Eva peccatrice, [8]
'Til Our Lord was a-born

De te genitrice. [9]
With '*ave*' it went away [10]
Dark the night, then comes the day
Salutatis; [11]
The well springeth out of thee
Virtutis. [12]

Well He knows He is thy son,
Ventre quem portasti; [13]
He will deny thee no boon,
Parvum quem locasti [14]
So gracious and so good he is,
To have brought us to bliss
Superni [15]
And has shut the foul pit
Inferni. [16]

In time of trouble, thy counsel the best,
Felix fecundata; [17]
From all weariness thou bringest rest,
Mater honorata. [18]
Beseech him with gentle heart
Who for us his blood did part
In cruce [19]
That we may come to him
In luce. [20]

---

1. Like a star seen at sea. 2. A virgin, but with a child. 3. So holy. 4. Rose
without thorns. 5. Through divine grace. 6 Chosen as queen of paradise.
7. Gentle maiden, made into a mother. 8. All the world was lost through
Eve's sin. 9. Through thee his mother. 10. Ave = hail. 11. Health-bringer.
12. From thy virtue. 13. Carried in thy womb. 14. Given to thee when small.
15. Celestial. 16. Of hell. 17. Blessed fruitfulness. 18. Highly favoured mother.
19. On the Cross. 20. In light.

St Thomas Aquinas 1225-1274
(translated by Fr Gerard Manley Hopkins)

Adoro Te Supplex, Latens Deitas – Godhead Here in Hiding

Godhead here in hiding, whom I do adore
Masked by these bare shadows, shape and nothing more,
See, Lord, at thy service low lies here a heart
Lost, all lost in wonder at the God thou art.

Seeing, touching, tasting are in thee deceived;
How says trusty hearing? that shall be believed;
What God's Son has told me, take for truth I do;
Truth himself speaks truly or there's nothing true.

On the cross thy godhead made no sign to men;
Here thy very manhood steals from human ken:
Both are my confession, both are my belief
And I pray the prayer of the dying thief.

I am not like Thomas, wounds I cannot see,
But can plainly call thee Lord and God as he:
This faith each day deeper be my holding of,
Daily make me harder hope and dearer love.

O thou our reminder of Christ crucified
Living Bread the life of us for whom he died,
Lend this life to me then: feed and feast my mind,
There he thou the sweetness man was meant to find.

Bring the tender tale true of the Pelican;[1]
Bathe me, Jesu Lord, in what thy bosom ran –
Blood that but one drop of has the world to win
All the world forgiveness of its world of sin.

Jesu whom I look at shrouded here below,
I beseech thee send me what I thirst for so,
Some day to gaze on thee face to face in light
And be blest for ever with thy glory's sight.

---

1. According to legend the pelican fed its young by pecking at its breast until its blood ran down for them to drink.

St Thomas Aquinas (1225-74)
(translated by J.M. Neale, E. Caswall and others)

O Salutaris Hostia – O Saving Victim

> O saving victim, opening wide
> The gate of heaven to man below;
> Our foes press on from every side;
> Thine aid supply, thy strength bestow.
>
> To thy great name be endless praise,
> Immortal Godhead, one in three,
> O grant us endless length of days
> In our true native land with thee.
> Amen.

Tantum Ergo Sacramentum – Therefore We, Before Him Bending

> Therefore we, before him bending,
> This great sacrament revere;
> Types and shadows have their ending,
> For the newer rite is here;
> Faith, our outward sense befriending,
> Makes the inward vision clear.
>
> Glory let us give, and blessing
> To the Father and the Son,
> Honour, might, and praise addressing,
> While eternal ages run;
> Ever too his love confessing
> Who from both, with both is one.
> Amen.

Anonymous c1250 (translated by Russell Sparkes)

Wait a While

> O Lord, Thou that calledst me,
> I have not yet answered Thee,

Except in words slow and sleepy;
'Wait yet! Just a little while!'
But 'yet' and 'yet' was endless,
And 'a little while' lasts for ever.

Anonymous c1250 (translated by Russell Sparkes)

Stand Firm, Mother!

'Stand firm, Mother, beneath the cross,
Behold thy child with joyful heart,
Blessed mother that thou art.'
'Son, how may I joyful stand,
I see thy feet, I see thy hand,
Nailed to the cursed tree.'

'Mother, away with thy weeping,
I suffer this death for Man's sin,
My own sins bear I none.'
'Son, I feel the death-wound,
As foretold to me by Simeon.'

'Mother, mercy upon thy child!
Wash away thy bloody tears,
They pain me more than death.'
'Son, how may I end my tears?
I see thy blood in rivers run,
From thy heart down to thy feet.'

'Mother, must I to thee do tell,
If I do not die, thou goest to Hell!
I suffer this death for thy sake.'
'Son, my mind is feebled with thy pain,
Blame me not for a mother's heart,
That these floods of tears do make.'

'Mother, mercy let me die!
So Adam free from Hell may be,

Else all mankind is lost.'
'Son, what am I to do?
Seeing thy torment torments me so,
Oh, let me die before thee.'

'Mother, now shalt thou learn,
The pains of those who children bear,
The sorrows of those who children lose.'
'Son, I feel it, let me tell,
Unless it were the pains of Hell,
Greater sorrow I could not know.'

'Mother, have pity on a mother's woe!
Now a mother's fate shalt thou know,
Even pure maiden that thou art.'
'Son, help all those in need,
All those who to me do grieve,
Maiden, wife, all women's heart'

'Mother, on this earth no longer may I dwell,
The time is come, I go to Hell,
But the third day I shall rise again.'
'Son, let me go with thee,
I am surely dying from thy wounds
So dreadful a death was never known.'

Richard Rolle c1290-1349
(translated by Russell Sparkes)

Love is Life

Love is life that e'er will last,
When in Christ it is fixed fast;
No joy nor woe may change it,
As the wisest men have writ.
The night is turned into day,
All work made into rest;
Let thou love, as I thee say,
So thou may live with the blessed.

Love is thought with great desire
Of the most fair beloved;
Life is likened to a fire
That may never be extinguished.
Love shall clean us of sin,
Love our remedy shall bring;
Love the king's heart may win,
Love for joy's sake may sing.

The seat of love is set on high,
Up to Heaven does it run;
On earth it seems to go awry,
It makes man pale and wan.
To the love of God it goes on nigh,
I tell thee from my own mind's eye;
Though the way to us may tire,
It is through love that God and man unite.

Love is hotter than burning coal,
Love may never be deceived;
No man may hold the flame of love –
Its constant, burning heat.
Love restores us to health,
And raises us up to Heaven.
Love through Christ bursts into our hearts,
I know no joy to compare.

Learn to love, if live thou wilt,
When this earth thou must leave.
Hold thy thoughts on Him
Who mayst keep thee from care.
See that thy heart does not depart
From Him, though wandering it wishes to go;
So thou may win Him with joy,
And love Him for evermore.

Jesus, Thou that gave life to me,
Let me to Thee my sweet love bring;
All my wants take up to Thee,
Let this be all my longing;
Then woe away from me will be,
And present all my desiring;
As long as my soul doth hear and heed
The song of Thy praising.

Life with Thee lasteth for ever,
From the time that we may feel it;
Make me burn with inner fire,
So nothing may cool it.
Take my thoughts in hand,
And make my doubts fast;
Let me not to this world's good things,
Be as a slave and in thrall.

Were I to love an earthly thing
Most pleasing to my will,
The core of my joy and longing,
When it shall come to me;
I'll know fear of its loss,
Fear hot and full of pain.
For all my wealth is but weeping,
When torment shall burn my soul.

The joy that men have seen,
Is likened to the hay;
That once was fresh and green,
And now is withered away.
Such is this world, I know,
It shall be so 'til Doomsday;
Man lives in toil and sorrow –
None may escape, try they may.

If thou lov'st with all thy thought,
And hate the filth of sin,
And give thy heart to Him it brought,
Inner joy will grow within.
For thy soul Christ has sought,
In His quest without an end;
Thou shalt to bliss be brought,
And dwell with Him in Heaven.

The test of love is this,
That it is faithful and true;
It stands firm in steadiness,
Not restless for something new.
The life that love might find,
Whoever by heart it knew,
Finds himself freed from care,
On the path to joy and bliss.

Thus I bid thee love Christ,
As I have told thee so;
With angels thou shalt take thy place,
Exchange that joy for nothing.
On earth have no foe
Unless he could cast down thy love;
For love is as strong as death,
Love is as hard as Hell.

Love is a light burden,
Love gladdens both young and old;
Love feels no pain,
As lovers have often told.
Love is a wine for the spirit,
That makes man brave and bold;
Through love no one can lose,
Who love in his heart does hold.

Love is the sweetest thing,
That man on earth can own;
Love is God's darling,
Love binds blood and bone.
In love shall be all our living,
I know no better home;
For me and my desiring,
Love makes both be one.

But fleshy love shall fail,
As do flowers in May;
There is no strength in it,
It lasteth but one day.
And sorrow follows for sure,
Both pride and the passion play;
When lovers are cast down,
To torment that lasts for ever.

When earth and air shall burn,
Then shall they fear and shake,
And men shall rise up,
To answer for their deeds.
If they have been in sin,
In the life that now they lead;
They shall be shut up in Hell,
With darkness as their reward.

Rich men shall wring their hands,
And pay for their wicked works;
In flames of fire knight and king
With sorrow and shame shall lie.
If thou wilt love, then to Christ
Most melodiously do sing;
The love of Him overcomes all,
For in love we live and die.

A Song of the Passion

My truest treasure so treacherously was taken;
So bitterly bound with biting bands.
How soon from Thy servants Thou wert forsaken,
For my sake reluctant snatched from their hands.

The well-spring of my well-being, so terribly twisted,
So pushed out of prison to Pilate at prime.[1]
Their blows and curses quietly Thou suffered,
When they spat in Thy face saliva and slime.

My hope of healing, hurried to be hanged,
So burdened with Thy cross, so crowned with thorns;
Hateful to Thy heart, Thy steps they jeered,
Thy back must surely break, but it bends forlorn.

Saviour of my soul, so sorrowful in sight,
So naked and nailed, Thy back on the rood, [2]
Full hideously hanging, they heaved Thee up high,
The cross placed in the stone that there ready stood.

My heart's desire, so dreadfully disposed,
So stretched upright, straining on the rood;
For all Thy great meekness, mercy, and might,
Thou curest all my ills with the gift of Thy blood.

Shield from my foes, of proven renown,
So gently descending, when evening came;
Thy mother and her friends let Thee down,
All there wept to see Thy wounds so deep.

My prince without peer, to Thee I pray,
My mind of this vision let me never miss;
But firm my will to live with Thee forever,
Be Thou buried in my heart and bring me to bliss.
Amen

1. Prime = dawn. 2. Rood = cross.

Anonymous c1300 (translated by Russell Sparkes)

Judas

It was Maundy Thursday when Our Lord arose,
Gently these words to Judas he spoke:

'Judas, thou must to Jerusalem to purchase our fare,
Thirty pieces of silver on thy back shalt thou bear.
Thou shalt come to the broad street, to the broad street,
Some of thy kinsmen there shalt thou meet.'

He met there with his sister, a shameless woman,
'Judas, thou should be pelted with stone, pelted with stone,
On behalf of that false prophet thou believest in.'

'Hold thy tongue, dear sister, lest thy false heart
   should break,
If my Lord Jesus knew, vengeance on thee would
   he wreak.'

'Judas, go up the rock, high upon the stone,
Lay thy head on my lap, and sleep thee anon.'

When Judas from sleep did awake,
Thirty pieces of silver from him they did take.
He tore his hair, 'til it flowed with blood,
The Jews believed that there a madman stood.

Came forth to him the rich Jew named Pilatus:
'Wilt thou sell thy lord, him called Jesus?'

'I'll sell my Lord for no coins of gold,
But only the silver he gave me to hold.'
'Wilt thou sell thy lord for coins of any kind?'
'Nay, but only for the silver that was mine.'

....

In came Our Lord, the apostles at their meat:
'Why sit ye, apostles, why needs ye eat?
Why sit ye, apostles, why needs ye eat?
Today I am bought and sold for our meat.'

Up then stood Judas: 'Lord, is it me?
No man has heard me speak evil of Thee?'

Up then stood Peter, who spoke with all his might:
'Though Pilatus should come with the strongest knight,
Though Pilatus should come with the strongest knight,
I will, dear Lord, for thy sake fight.'

'Be still, Peter, of thee I well know,
Thou shalt forsake me, ere the cock thrice shall crow.'

Anonymous c1300 (translated by Russell Sparkes)

Deo Gracias (Thanks be to God)

In a church where I did kneel,
The other day one morning,
I liked the service wondrous well,
The longer then my tarrying.
I saw a priest a book forth bring,
That music on its pages has,
Quickly he sought the words to sing,
Which were *Deo Gracias.*

The singers in the choir, loud and clear
On that word rang their voices out,
The sound was good, and I drew near,
And called for a priest to make it out.
And said: 'Sir, for your courtesy,
Tell me, if I may ask,
What it means, and for why,
Do ye sing *Deo Gracias?'*

In silk that comely priest was clad,
And over a lectern leaned he;
And with his words he made me glad,
When he said: 'My son, I shall tell thee.
Father and Son in Trinity,
The Holy Ghost, ground of our grace,
Therefore, without cease, thank we,
As we say *Deo Gracias*.'

'To thank and bless him are we bound,
With all the joy that man may mind,
For the world in woe was wrapped and wound,
'Til he crept into mankind,
To a lady most high he stepped within,
The worthiest that ever was,
And shed his precious blood for our sin,
So sing we *Deo Gracias*.'

Then said the priest: 'Son, by thy leave,
I must now go to say my service,
I pray thee do not take offence,
For thou has heard it plain,
This is why it is clerks practice,
And Holy Church within the Mass,
Unto our Saviour, Prince of Peace,
For to sing, *Deo Gracias*.'

From out that church I went on my way,
But these words were always in my thought,
And to myself twenty times did say:
'God grant that I forget it not.
Though to trouble I may be brought,
What help were it to say "alas"?
I shall but say "*Deo Gracias*".'

Anonymous c1300 (translated by Russell Sparkes)

This World's Goods Are Fantasy

From what is man, and for what?
Who knows if he be ought or nought?
From earth and air grow up a gnat,
And so for man, when truth is sought.
Though man become great and fat,
He melts away just like a moth.

Man's might is but of little worth,
But hurts him and turns to nought.
Who knows, but He who all things hath wrought,
What becomes of man when he shall die,
Who knows of death except by fancy thought,
For this world's goods are fantasy.

Men die, and beasts die,
And all seems by chance,
And both from death must die,
Yet they live but once.
Save that men have more wit,
Between them is no difference.

Who knows if men's soul shall rise up,
And if beasts' souls shall sink down?
Who understands the speech of beasts,
When to their creator they do cry?
Only God understands their sound,
For this world's goods are fantasy.

Anonymous c1350 (translated by Russell Sparkes)

I Sing of a Maiden

I sing of a maiden
Who no man did know;
The King of all kings
As her son she chose.

He came all so still
Where His mother was,
As dew in April
That falleth on the grass.

He came all so still
To His mother's bower,
As dew in April
That falleth on the flower.

He came all so still,
Where His mother lay
As dew in April
That falleth on the spray.

Mother and maiden
Was never such but she;
Well may such a lady
God's mother truly be.

William Langland c1330-1395
(translated by Russell Sparkes)

A Vision of Holy Church
(Piers Plowman, *extract from Book One*)

(The author falls asleep on the Malvern Hills, and has a vision of
a wonderful tower built on a mountain, of a dark abyss with a
dungeon in it, and between them a great plain full of people
occupied with worldly affairs. A beautiful woman, Holy Church,
appears to him.)

The meaning of this mountain, and of the dark dale
And the field full of folk, I shall now make plain.
A lady clothed in linen, and fair of face,
Came down from the castle and called to me gently:
'My son, why sleepest thou? Seest thou these people,
How busy they be in the turmoil of trade?

The most part of people who pass through this earth,
Worship the things of this world; they want naught else.
Of Heaven on high they take no account.'

Her face frightened me, though mild was her manner,
So I asked: 'Grant pardon, lady, but what does this mean?'
'The tower on high,' answered she, 'holds Truth therein.
His will is for you to act as His words have taught –
For He is the father of faith and creator of all.
It was He who gave you mind and body, five senses
To worship Him with when living on earth below.
Therefore he told the earth to provide wool, linen,
    and food,
Enough for all to live on, who live in moderation.'

'He commanded from his kindness three things should be
    in common;
Nought is needed but these, now hear them in order:
The first is clothing, to keep you from the cold,
Then food to eat, to hold you from hunger,
And drink when thy throat is dry, but not too much-
So that your work the worse for it shall not be.[1]
Remember Lot in his lifetime, whose love of drink
Led him to dance with his daughters to the Devil's delight.
He drowned himself in drink, became the Devil's tool,
Was caught in the toils of lechery, and slept with them both;
Witless with wine, he did the wicked deed:
Inebriemus eum vino, dormiamsque cum eo
Ut servare possimus de patre nostro semen.[2]
Through women and wine was Lot overwhelmed
And so begot in gluttony children accursed.'

'So forswear the delights of drink for thine own sake;
Moderation is the best medicine, ignore thy cravings.
The stomach's sweetness is not that of the soul;
Food for the flesh does not sustain the spirit.
Believe not the body, it will lead thee astray,
The flesh and the Devil work together.

They seek thy soul lying deep in thy heart –
Be wary, I warn thee, I warrant it is for the best.'

'Good lady,' said I, 'I give thanks for your words so wise.[3]
Now tell me, the wealth of this world, that men cling to,
To whom does this great treasure truly belong?'
'Go to the Gospel,' she replied, 'that God Himself spoke,
When the people in the temple asked Him of a penny,
Whether they should worship Caesar's face thereon?
And God asked them: what image, and whose name
Was written upon the face of the coin.
"*Caesar*," they said,"is the name written plain."
"*Reddite Cesari*," said God, "what belongs to *Cesari*,"[4]
Et que sunt dei, deo, or you will do ill."
For right reasoning should rule you all;
Let natural wisdom be warden of your wealth –
The trustee of your treasure, to be ready at need,
For good management and good sense go together.'

Then I asked her softly, by the name of Him who
      founded her:
'That dungeon in the deep, so dreadful a sight,
I beseech ye, Lady, what does it mean?'
'That is the castle of sorrow; whoever enters there
Shall curse the day that he was born.
There dwells a creature called Wrong,
Father of falsehood, creator of the castle.
Adam and Eve he urged to evil,
Counselled Cain to kill his brother,
Judas he trapped with the Jews' silver,
Then got him hanged on an elder tree.
He is the enemy of Love, though he loves to lie;
All who trust in his treasure shall be betrayed.'

Then I wondered in my mind what woman this was
To explain Holy Writ so wisely and so well.
And I asked, in His Holy Name, before her going hence
Who it was who taught me so kindly?

'I am Holy Church,' replied she, 'as thou shouldst know.
I baptised thee as a baby, instructed thee in the Faith;
Thou camest to me with promises of my will to perform,
And to love me loyally for the length of thy life.'

Then I fell to my knees, and cried to her for mercy,
And prayed for pity, and pardon for my sins.
And grace to help me understand, in Christ to believe.
That I might work His will who made me man:
'Teach me of no earthly treasure, but tell me the way
To save my soul, as the saints assert.'

'When all treasure is tested,' she said, 'Truth is the best.
Let the text *deus caritas* be judged as proof. [5]
We should be as dearly devoted to her as to dear God
    Himself.
Whoever speaks only the truth, and says naught else,
And does good works, and wishes no man ill,
Is like Our Lord, a god in heaven and on earth.'

....

'So I say again, as before, that Truth is best.
Let the unlettered learn it, the learned know it well,
That truth is the choicest treasure to be found on earth.'
'But I have no talent for understanding,' I said, 'you must
    teach me better,
Whence comes conscience, where it is to be found?'
'Thou dull dolt,' she replied, 'dense indeed are thy wits!
How little Latin thou must have learned in thy youth;
Heu mihi, quod sterilem duxi vitam iuvenilem! [6]
There is nature's law that is true teacher to thy heart:
Love Our Lord with more longing than thyself,
Avoid mortal sin, even at the cost of death.
This I swear is Truth; if any can teach thee better,
Pay heed to his words and learn them by heart.
This is the witness of His word, words that thou must
    follow:

For Truth tells that Love is Heaven's remedy.
Use this medicine to keep thee spotless from sin.
According to His will God wrought all His works with
    Love,
And taught Moses that it was the nearest thing to Heaven,
The plant of peace, most precious of virtues.
So heavy it was, that Heaven could not hold it
'Till of earth it had eaten its fill,
To take on flesh and blood from this world.
Sharp and quick moving as the point of a needle
Neither armour nor high walls can hinder it.

Therefore Love leads Our Lord's people in Heaven –
A mediator, like a mayor between king and people.
Just so is Love our leader and shaper of the law,
Who metes out fines for men's misdeeds.
To know her intimately, let her come with might
Into thy heart; then shalt thou be devout.
For the heart's assent is a mighty beginning
That falls to the Father who formed us all;
Looked on with love, and let His Son die
Meekly for our misdeeds, to heal us all.
And yet He willed not woe for those who tormented
    Him so,
But meekly with His own mouth asked for mercy
For pity on the people who put Him to death.
Here may thou see examples of His love
That He was mighty but meek, and mercy gave
To those who hung Him high and pierced His heart.

1. In the Middle Ages weak beer was a staple drink, as water was often impure.
2. The Vulgate, Genesis 19:32 'Come let us make our father drink wine, and we will lie with him, so that we may preserve offspring through our father.'
3. In Middle English, an equal or inferior was addressed as 'thou', a superior as 'you', so the dreamer calls Holy Church 'you'.
4. Matthew 22:20-22 'Give therefore to Caesar the things that are Caesar's, and to God the things that are God's.'
5. Deus caritas = God is love.
6. Woe is me for my barren and wasted youth!

Geoffrey Chaucer c1343-1400

Ballad of Good Counsel

Flee from the press, and dwell with soothfastness, [1]
Suffice unto thy good, though it be small; [2]
For hoard hath hate, and climbing tickleness, [3]
Press hath envy, and weal blent overall. [4]
Savour no more than thee behove shall;
Rule well thyself, that other folk canst rede; [5]
And Truth thee shall deliver, it is no dread.

Temper thee nought all crooked to redress,
In trust of her that turneth as a ball:
Great rest stands in little busyness;
Be ware also to spurn against an awl; [6]
Strive not, as does the crock with the wall.
Daunt thyself, that dauntest others' deeds; [7]
And Truth thee shall avail, it is no dread.

That thee is sent, receive in buxomness, [8]
The wrestling for this world asketh a fall.
Here is no home, here is naught but a wilderness:
Forth, pilgrim, forth! Forth, beast, out of thy stall!
Know thy country, look up, thank God of all;
Hold the highway, and let thy ghost thee lead;
And Truth thee shall deliver, it is no dread.

Envoi

Therefore, thou Vache, leave thine old wretchedness [9]
Unto the world; leave now to be thrall;
Cry him mercy, that of his high goodness
Made thee of nought, and in especial
Draw unto him, and pray in general
For thee, and even for other, heavenly meed; [10]
And Truth thee shall deliver, it is no dread.

1. Press, etc – flee from the crowd, and live with honesty. 2. Be content with thy lot. 3. Climbing tickleness = worldly success is uncertain. 4. Weal blent = riches blind. 5. Rede = advice. 6. Ignore the pinpricks of life. 7. Daunt = overcome. 8. Accept what fate sends you. 9. Vache = cow, metaphorically the animal lethargy of the body. 10. Meed = reward.

A Poor Parson

A good man was there of religion,
And was a poor parson of a town,
But rich he was of holy thought and work.
He was also a learned man, a clerk,
That Christ's gospel truly would he preach;
His parishens devoutly would he teach. [1]
Benign he was, and wonder diligent,
And in adversity full patient,
And such he was proved often sithes. [2]
Full loath were him to cursen for his tithes,
But rather would he given, out of doubt
Unto his poorer parishens about
Of his offering and eke of his substance. [3]
He could in little thing have suffisance.
Wide was his parish, and houses far asunder,
But he none left not, for rain nor thunder,
In sickness nor in mischief to visite
The farthest in his parish much and lite, [4]
Upon his feet, and in his hand a stave.
This noble example to his sheep he gave
That first he wrought and afterward he taught.
Out of the gospel he the words caught;
And this figure he added thereto,
That if gold rust, what shall iron do?
For if a priest be foul, on whom we trust,
No wonder is a lewd man to rust;
And shame it is, if a priest take keep,
A filthy shepherd and a clean sheep. [5]
Well ought a priest example for to give,
By his cleanness, how his sheep should live.
He set not his benefice to hire
And left his sheep encumbered in the mire
And ran to London unto St Paul's
To seeken him a chantry for souls,
Or with a brotherhood to be withhold;
But dwelt at home, and kept well his fold,

So that the wolf ne'er made it not miscarry;
He was a shepherd and not a mercenary.
And though he holy were and virtuous,
He was to sinful men not despitous,[6]
Nor of his speech dangerous nor digne,[7]
But in his teaching discreet and benign.
To drawen folk to heaven by fairness,
By good example, this was his business.
But it were any person obstinate,
What so he were, of high or low estate,
Him would he snibben sharply for the nonce.[8]
A better priest I trow that nowhere none is.
He waited after no pomp and reverence,
Nor maked him a spiced conscience, [9]
But Christ's lore and his apostles' twelve
He taught, but first he followed it himself.

1. Parishens = parishioners. 2. Sithes = times. 3. Eek = even. 4. Much and lite
= mighty and humble. 5. I have substituted 'filthy' for a more vulgar epithet.
6. Despitous = despising. 7. Digne = haughty. 8. He would rebuke. 9. He was
not over-scrupulous, did not concern himself with trifles.

Prologue to *The Second Nun's Tale*

Thou maid and mother, daughter of thy Son,
Thou well of mercy, sinful soul's cure
In whom that God, for bounty, chose to wone,[1]
Thou humble and high over every creature,
Thou didst so far ennoble our nature
That no disdain the Maker had of kind
His Son in Blood and Flesh to clothe and wind.

Within the blissful cloister of thy sides
Took man's shape the Eternal Love and Peace
That of the Trine compass Lord and guide is
Whom earth and sea and heaven, without cease
For ever praise; and thou, Virgin, spotless,
Bore of thy body, and dweltest maiden pure,
The Creator of every creature.

Assembled is in thee magnificence
With mercy, goodness, and with such pity
That thou that art the sum of excellence
Not only helpest them that pray to thee
But often time, of thy benignity
Full freely, ere that men thy help beseech
Thou goest before, thy healing hand to reach.

Now help, thou meek and fair and blissful maid,
Me, exiled in this wilderness of gall.
Think on that woman by the well who said
Even the dogs may eat the crumbs, ay, all
That from their lord's table sometime fall;
And though that I, unworthy son of Eve,
Be sinful, yet accept thou my belief.

1. Wone = live, inhabit.

The Prioress' Tale (extract) (modernised by Wordsworth)

O Lord, our Lord! how wondrously, (quoth she)
Thy name in this large world is spread abroad!
For not alone by men of dignity
Thy worship is performed and precious laud.
But by the mouths of children, gracious God!
Thy goodness is set forth; they when they lie
Upon the breast thy name do glorify.

Wherefore in praise, the worthiest that I may,
Jesu! of thee, and the white Lily-flower
Which did thee bear, and is a Maid for aye,
To tell a story I will use my power;
Not that I may increase her honour's dower,
For she herself is honour, and the root
Of goodness, next her Son, our soul's best boot.[1]

O Mother Maid! O Maid and Mother free!
O bush unburnt! burning in Moses' sight!
That down didst ravish from the Deity,
Through humbleness, the spirit that did alight

Upon thy heart, whence, through that glory's might,
Conceived was the Father's sapience,
Help me to tell it in thy reverence!

Lady! thy goodness, thy magnificence,
Thy virtue, and thy great humility,
Surpass all science and all utterance;
For sometimes, Lady! ere men pray to thee
Thou goest before in thy benignity,
The light to us vouchsafing of thy prayer,
To be our guide unto thy Son so dear.

My knowledge is so weak, O blissful Queen!
To tell abroad thy mighty worthiness,
That I the weight of it may not sustain;
But as a child of twelve months old or less,
That laboreth his language to express,
Even so fare I; and therefore, I thee pray,
Guide thou my song which I of thee shall say.

1. Middle English *bote* – cure, remedy.

Fr John Audelay c1360-1430
(translated by Russell Sparkes)

*Timor Mortis Conturbat Me – Passio Christi Conforta Me
(The fear of death confounds me – the passion of Christ
consoles me)*

Our Lady help! Jesus mercy!
Timor mortis conturbat me.

Dread of death, sorrow of sin,
Trouble my heart most grievously;
Past lusts unsettle the soul within –
Passio Christi conforta me.

For blindness is a heavy thing,
To be deaf too a double difficulty,

To lose my sight and my hearing –
Passio Christi conforta me.

To lose the sense of taste and smell,
Constantly sick in my body;
The body's pleasures bid farewell-
Passio Christi conforta me.

Thus God He gives and takes away,
And, as He will, so must it be.
His name be blessed both night and day –
Passio Christi conforta me.

Here is a cause of great mourning:
Of myself I nothing see
But filth, uncleanness, vile stinking-
Passio Christi conforta me.

In this world I nothing brought,
Nothing shall take away with me;
Save good deeds, words, and thought-
Passio Christi conforta me.

The five wounds of Jesus Christ
My medicine now must be,
The devil's power down to cast-
Passio Christi conforta me.

As I lay sick in my weakness,
With sorrow of heart and tear of eye,
This carol I made with great sadness –
Passio Christi conforta me.

Oft with this prayer I me blessed:
'In manus tuas, Domine'; [1]
Take my soul into thy rest –
Passio Christi conforta me.

Mary, mother, merciful maid;
For the joy thou haddest, lady,
Pray thy Son for me to aid –
Passio Christi conforta me.

Learn this lesson from blind Audelay:
When pain is greatest, near cure may be.
If thou art troubled night or day,
Say: *'Passio Christi conforta me.'*

1. 'Into thy hands, Lord': cf Luke 23:46.

Anonymous c1400 (translated by Russell Sparkes)

Our Lady's Lullaby

Jesus, sweetest son so dear,
On a pitiful bed thou liest here
And that me grieveth sore;
For thy cradle is a byre,
Oxen and asses be thy squire:
Weep I must therefore.

Jesus, sweet son, be not wrath
That I have neither rug nor cloth
Around thee for to fold;
For I have no cloth to wrap:
But lay thy head on my lap
And hide thee from the cold.

Anonymous c1400

Adam Lay a-Bounden

Adam lay a-bounden[1]
Bounden in a bond;
Four thousand winter
Thought he not too long.
And all was for an apple,

An apple that he took,
As clerks finden
Written in their book.

Ne'er had the apple taken been,
The apple taken been,
Ne'er had never Our Lady
A been Heaven's Queen.
Blessed be the time
That apple taken was!
Therefore we must singen,
'Deo Gracias!'[2]

1. In bondage to sin. 2. Thanks be to God!

Fr John Lydgate c1370-1451

Tarry No Longer

Tarry no longer toward thine heritage,
Hasten on thy way, and be of right good cheer.
Go each day onward on thy pilgrimage;
Think how short time thou shalt abide here!
Thy place is built above the stars full clear,
No earthly palace wrought in so stately wise.
Come on, My friend, My brother most entire!
For thee I offered My blood in sacrifice.

Let Devout People Keep Observance

Ye devout people which keep one observance,
Meekly in church to kiss stone or tree,
Earth or iron, hath in remembrance
What they doth mean and take the morality;
Earth is clear token of the humanity
Of Christ Jesu; the stone, the sepulchre;
The spear of steel, the sharp nails three
Caused his five wounds remembered in scripture.

Think on the cross made of iv divers trees,
As clerks do say, cedar and cypress,
To high estates, to folk of low degrees,
Christ brought inner peace, the olive beareth witness,
Namely when virtue conserveth his greenness;
Look on these signs and have them in memory,
And how the palm configured his victory.

These iv figures, combined into one,
Set on thy mind for a memorial;
Earth and iron, four trees, and the stone,
To make us free, whereas we were in thrall;
Behold the banner, victorious and royal!
Christ's cross, a standard of most peace;
Think how the thief for mercy did call,
Taught by the tree the way to paradise!

Your hearts ye lift up into the east,
And all your body and knees bow a-down,
When the priest sayeth *verbum caro factum est*,[1]
With all your inward contemplation,
Your mouth first cross with high devotion,
Kissing the token rehearsed here before,
And ever have in mind Christ's passion,
Which for thy sake wore a crown of thorns.

1. *Verbum caro factum est* = the Word was made flesh.

François Villon 1431-1485?
(translated by D.G. Rossetti)

His Mother's Prayer to Our Lady

Lady of Heaven and earth, and therewithal
Crowned Empress of the nether clefts of Hell –
I, thy poor Christian, on thy name do call –
Commending me to thee, with thee to dwell,
Albeit in nought I be commendable.

But all mine undeserving may not mar
Such mercies as thy sovereign mercies are;
Without the which (as true words testify)
No soul can reach thy Heaven so fair and far.
Even in this faith I choose to live and die.

Unto thy Son say thou that I am
And to me graceless make Him gracious.
Sad Mary of Egypt lacked not of that bliss,
Nor yet the sorrowful clerk Theophilus,
Whose bitter sins were set aside even thus
Though to the Fiend his bounden service was.
Oh, help me, lest in vain for me should pass
(Sweet Virgin that shalt have no loss thereby!)
The blessed Host and sacring of the Mass.
Even in this faith I choose to live and die.

A pitiful poor woman, shrunk and old,
I am, and nothing learned in letter-lore.
Within my parish-cloister I behold
A painted heaven where harps and lutes adore,
And eke an Hell whose damned folk seethe full sore:
One bringeth fear, the other joy to me.
That joy, great Goddess, make thou mine to be –
Thou of whom all must ask it even I;
And that which faith desires, that let it see.
For in this faith I choose to live and die.

Envoi

O excellent Virgin Princess! thou didst bear
King Jesus, the most excellent comforter,
Who even of this our weakness craved a share.
And for our sake stooped to us from on high,
Offering to death His young life sweet and fair.
Such as He is, Our Lord, I Him declare,
And in this faith I choose to live and die.

François Villon 1431-1485? (translated by A.C. Swinburne)

Epitaph made by Villon whilst expecting to be hanged

Men, brother men, that after us yet live,
Let not your hearts too hard against us be;
For if some pity of us poor men ye give,
The sooner God shall take of you pity.
Here are we five or six strung up, you see,
And here the flesh that all too well we fed
Bit by bit eaten and rotten, rent and shred,
And we the bones grow dust and ash withal;
Let no man laugh at us discomforted,
But pray to God that he forgive us all.

If we call on you, brothers, to forgive,
Ye should not hold our prayer in scorn, though we
Were slain by law; ye know that all alive
Have not wit always to walk righteously;
Make therefore intercession heartily
With him that of a virgin's womb was bred,
That his grace be not as a dry well-bed
For us, nor let hell's thunder on us fall:
We are dead, let no man harry or vex us dead,
But pray to God that he forgive us all.

The rain has washed and laundered us all five,
And the sun dried and blackened; yea perdie,
Ravens and pies with beaks that rend and rive
Have dug our eyes out, and plucked off for fee
Our beards and eyebrows; never are we free,
Not once, to rest; but here and there still sped,
Drive at its wild will by the wind's change led,
More pecked of birds than fruits on garden-wall;
Men, for God's love, let no gibe here be said,
But pray to God that he forgive us all.

Envoi

Prince Jesus, that of all art Lord and head,
Keep us, that hell be not our bitter bed;
We have nought to do in such a master's hall.
Be not ye therefore of our fellowhead,
But pray to God that he forgive us all.

Fr John Skelton 1460-1529

To the Second Person

O benign Jesu, my sovereign Lord and King,
The only Son of God by filiation,
The Second Person withouten beginning,
Both God and man, our faith maketh plain relation,
Mary Thy mother, by way of incarnation,
Whose glorious passion our souls doth revive,
Against all bodily and ghostly tribulation
Defend me with Thy piteous wounds five.

O peerless Prince, pained to the death,
Ruefully rent, Thy body wan and blo, [1]
For my redemption gave up Thy vital breath,
Was never sorrow like to Thy deadly woe!
Grant me, out of this world when I shall go,
Thine endless mercy for my preservative:
Against the world, the flesh, the devil also,
Defend me with Thy piteous wounds five.

1. Blo = pale, bloodless.

Meditation upon the Gift of a Skull (sent to him by a lady)

Your ugly token
My mind hath broken
From worldly lust:
For I have discussed
We are but dust,

81

And die we must.
It is general
To be mortal:
I have well espied
No man may him hide!
From Death hollow-eyed,
With sinews withered,
With bones shivered,
With his worm-eaten maw,
And his ghastly jaw
Gasping aside,
Naked of hide,
Neither flesh nor fell. [1]
Then, by my counsel,
Look that ye spell
Well this gospel:
For whereso we dwell
Death will us quell,
And with us mell. [2]
For all our pampered paunches
There may no fraunchis, [3]
Nor worldly bliss,
Redeem us from this:
Our days be dated
To be check-mated
With draughts of death
Stopping our breath:
Our eyes sinking,
Our bodies stinking,
Our gums grinning,
Our souls brinning. [4]
To whom, then, shall we sue,
For to have rescue,
But to sweet Jesu
On us then for to rue?
O goodly child
Of Mary mild,

Then be our shield!
That we be not exiled
To the dun dale
Of bootless bale, [5]
Nor to the lake
Of Fiend's blake. [6]
But grant us grace
To see thy Face,
And to purchase
Thine heavenly place,
And thy palace
Full of solace
Above the sky
That is so high,
Eternally
To behold and see
The Trinity!
Amen.
Mercy vous y. [7]

1. Fell = skin. 2. Mell = meddle. 3. Fraunchis = freedom, release.
4. Brinning = burning. 5. Bootless bale = inescapable evil. 6. Blake = blackness.
7. Thank you for this.

Vexilla Regis Prodeunt – (The King's banners are displayed)

Now sing we, as we were wont,
Vexilla regis prodeunt.

The King's banner on field is splayed. [1]
The Cross's mystery cannot be nayed. [2]
To whom our Saviour was betrayed,
And for our sake.
Thus saith he:
I suffer for thee,
My death I take.
Now sing we, as we were wont,
Vexilla regis prodeunt.

Behold my shanks, behold my knees,
Behold my head, arms, and thees,[3]
Behold of me nothing thou sees
But sorrow and pine: [4]
Thus was I spilt,
Man, for thy guilt,
And not for mine.
Now sing we, as we were wont,
Vexilla regis prodeunt.

Behold my body, how Jews it dong[5]
With knots of whipcord and scourges strong:
As streams of a well the blood outsprong
On every side.
The knots were knit
Right well with wit,
They made wounds wide.
Now sing we, as we were wont,
Vexilla regis prodeunt.

Man, understand now thou shall,
Instead of drink they gave me gall,
And eisell mingled therewithall,[6]
The Jews fell.
Those pains on me
I suffered for thee
To bring thee from hell.
Now sing we, as we were wont,
Vexilla regis prodeunt.

Now for thy life thou hast mislead,
Mercy to ask be thou not adread:
The least drop of blood that I for thee shed
Might cleanse thee soon
Of all the sin
The world within
If thou haddest done.

Now sing we, as we were wont,
Vexilla regis prodeunt.

Man, thou shalt now understand,
Of my head, both foot and hand,
Are four c. and five thousand
Wounds and Sixty;
Fifty and vii.
Were told full even
Upon my body.
Now sing we, as we were wont,
Vexilla regis prodeunt.

Sith I for love bought thee so dear,[7]
As thou may see thyself here,
I pray thee with a right good cheer
Love me again:
That it likes me
To suffer for thee
Now all this pain.
Now sing we, as we were wont,
Vexilla regis prodeunt.

I was more wrother with Judas[8]
For he would no mercy ask
Than I was for his trespass
When he me sold;
I was ever ready
To grant him mercy,
But he none wold.
Now sing we, as we were wont,
Vexilla regis prodeunt.

Lo, how I hold mine arms abroad,
Thee to receive ready yspread[9]
For the great love that I to thee had
Well may thou know.

Some love again
I would full fain
Thou wouldest to me show.
Now sing we, as we were wont,
Vexilla regis prodeunt.

For love I ask nothing of thee
But stand fast in faith and sin thou flee,
And pain to live in honesty[10]
Both night and day.
And thou shalt have bliss
That never shall miss
Withouten nay.[11]
Now sing we, as we were wont,
Vexilla regis prodeunt

Now, Jesu, for thy great goodness,
That for men suffered great hardness,
Save us from the devil's cruelness
And to bliss us send,
And grant us grace
To see Thy Face
Withouten end.
Now sing we, as we were wont,
Vexilla regis prodeunt

1. Splay = displayed. 2. Nayed = denied. 3. Thees = thighs. 4. Pine = agony,
torment. 5. Dong = struck. 6. Eisell = vinegar. 7. Sith = in truth. 8. Wrother =
wrath, anger. 9. Yspread = outspread. 10. Pain = strive. 11. Withouten nay =
without doubt.

William Dunbar c1460-1513? (translated by
Russell Sparkes)

*Surrexit Dominus de Sepulchro (The Lord is risen from
the tomb)*

Done is a battle with the dragon black,
Our champion Christ confounds all his force;

The gates of Hell are broken with a crack
The sign is raised triumphant of the Cross,
The devils tremble with hideous voice,
The souls are redeemed, and to bliss can go,
Christ with His blood our ransom does endorse:
Surrexit Dominus de sepulchro.

Fallen is the deadly dragon Lucifer,
The cruel serpent with the deadly sting,
The old foe lying with his teeth ajar,
With which to catch us he waits so long,
Thinking to grip us in his claws strong;
The merciful Lord would not that it were so,
He made him miss that goal:
Surrexit Dominus de sepulchro.

He for our sake suffered to be slain,
And down like a lamb in sacrifice lain,
But like a lion rose up again,
As if a giant raised Him on high.
In comes Aurora radiant and bright,
Aloft has gone the glorious Apollo,
The blissful day emerges from the night,
Surrexit Dominus de sepulchro.

The great victor has risen on high,
That for our fault to the death was wounded;
The sun of life is now shining bright,
And darkness flees, our faith is now refounded,
The knell of mercy from heaven is sounded,
Christians are delivered from their woe,
The Jews and their error are confounded:
Surrexit Dominus de sepulchro.

The foe has fled, the battle has ceased,
The prison broken, the jailers put to flight;
The war is over, confirmed is the peace,

The fetters opened, and the dungeon emptied
The ransom paid, the prisoners redeemed,
The field is won, overcome is the foe,
Taken is the treasure that he kept:
Surrexit Dominus de sepulchro.

Lament for the Poets (Timor mortis conturbat me –
The fear of death confounds me)
(translated by Russell Sparkes)

I that was in health and gladness
Am troubled now with great sickness
And feebled with infirmity –
Timor mortis conturbat me.

Our pleasure here is all but vainglory,
This false world is but transitory;
The flesh is weak, the Devil is sly –
Timor mortis conturbat me.

The state of man does change and vary,
Now sound, now sick, now blithe, now sorry,
Now dancing merry, now like to die –
Timor mortis conturbat me.

No state here on earth can stand secure;
As with the wind waves the wicker
So fails this world's vanity –
Timor mortis conturbat me.

Unto the death goes all Estates,
Princes, prelates and potentates,
Both rich and poor of all degree –
Timor mortis conturbat me.

He takes the knights into the field,
Fully armed with helm and shield;

Victor he is of all melee –
Timor mortis conturbat me.

That strong unmerciful tyrant
Takes, from the mother's breast,
The innocent suckling babe –
Timor mortis conturbat me.

He takes the champion in the fight,
The captain in the tower shut up tight,
The lady in the bower full of beauty –
Timor mortis conturbat me.

He spares no lord for his puissance,
No priest for his intelligence;
His awful stroke no man may flee –
Timor mortis conturbat me.

Artful magicians and astrologers,
Professors of logic and theology,
Get no help from conclusions wise –
Timor mortis conturbat me.

In medicine them that practise,
Leeches, surgeons and physicians,
Themselves from Death may not defend –
Timor mortis conturbat me.

I see the poets among the throng,
Here play their pageants, but soon are gone;
Not spared is their faculty –
Timor mortis conturbat me.

He has greedily devoured,
The noble Chaucer, of poets the flower,
The monk of Bury, and Gower all three –
Timor mortis conturbat me.

Since he has my brothers taken,
He will not let me live for long;
By force I must his next prey be –
Timor mortis conturbat me.

Since for the Death no remedy is there,
Best it is that we for Death prepare;
After our death that live may we –
Timor mortis conturbat me.

Anonymous c1500

Cumberland Lie – Wake Dirge

This aye night, this aye night,
Every night and all,
Fire and sleet and candle light,
And Christ receive thy soul.

When thou from hence away are passed,
Every night and all,
To Whinny-muir thou com'st at last;
And Christ receive thy soul.

If ever thou gavest hosen and shoon,[1]
Every night and all,
Sit thee down and put them on;
And Christ receive thy soul.

If hosen and shoon thou gavest none,
Every night and all,
The winds shall prick thee to the bare bone;
And Christ receive thy soul.

From Whinny-muir when thou may'st pass,
Every night and all,
To Bridge of Dread thou com'st at last;
And Christ receive thy soul.

From Bridge of Dread when thou mayst pass,
Every night and all,
To Purgatory fire thou com'st at last;
And Christ receive thy soul.

If ever thou gavest meat or drink,
Every night and all,
The fire shall never make thee shrink;
And Christ receive thy soul.

If meat or drink thou ne'er gavest none,
Every night and all,
The fire will burn thee to the bare bone;
And Christ receive thy soul.

This aye night, this aye night,
Every night and all,
Fire and sleet and candle light,
And Christ receive thy soul.

1. Gave leggings and shoes.

PART II

The Reformation
1535-1625

The Reformation probably caused the greatest upheaval to the lives of ordinary people since the Norman Conquest. Most people went along with the new order, but a small minority actively opposed it despite the prospect of brutal torture and hideous execution. One of the latter was the Jesuit Robert Southwell, a great poet in an era of great poets. Many others outwardly conformed, but gave strong hints of their beliefs. Shakespeare was probably among their number.

St Thomas More 1478-1535, martyr

Consider Well

Consider well that both by night and day
While we busily provide and care
For our disport, our revel and our play,
For pleasant melody and dainty fare,
Death stealeth on full slily; unaware
He lieth at hand and shall us all surprise,
We wot not when nor where nor in what wise. [1]

When fierce temptations threat thy soul with loss
Think on His Passion and the bitter pain,
Think on the mortal anguish of the Cross,
Think on Christ's blood let out at every vein,
Think of His precious heart all rent in twain
For thy redemption think all this was wrought,
Nor be that lost which He so dearly bought.

1. Wot = know.

A Prayer

Grant, I Thee pray, such heat into mine heart
That to this love of Thine may be equal;
Grant me from Satan's service to astart,
With whom me rueth so long to have been in thrall;
Grant me, good Lord and Creator of all,
The flame to quench of all sinful desire
And in Thy love set all mine heart afire.

That when the journey of this deadly life [1]
My silly ghost hath finished, and thence [2]
Departen must without his fleshly wife,
Alone into his Lord's high presence,
He may Thee find, O well of indulgence,
In Thy lordship not as a lord, but rather
As a very tender, loving father.

1. Deadly = mortal. 2. Ghost = spirit.

The Measure of the Love of God

If love be strong, hot, mighty and fervent,
There may no trouble, grief or sorrow fall,
But that the lover would be well content
All to endure and think it eke too small,
Though it were death, so he might therewithal
The joyful presence of that person get
On whom he hath his heart and love a-set.

Thus should of God the lover be content
Any distress or sorrow to endure,
Rather than to be from God absent,
And glad to die, so that he may be sure
By his departing hence for to procure,
After this valley dark, the heavenly light,
And of his love the glorious blessed sight.

Not only a lover content is in his heart
But coveteth eke and longeth to sustain
Some labour, incommodity, or smart,
Loss, adversity, trouble, grief or pain:
And of his sorrow, joyful is and fain,
And happy thinketh himself that he may take
Some misadventure for his lover's sake.

Thus shouldest thou, that lovest God also,
In thine heart wish, covet, and be glad
For him to suffer trouble, pain and woe:
For whom if thou be never so woe bestead,
Yet thou ne shalt sustain (be not adread)
Half the dolour, grief and adversity
That He already suffered hath for thee.

To Fortune (written in the Tower of London)

My flattering fortune, look thou never so fair,
Or never so pleasantly begin to smile,

As though thou wouldst my ruin all repair,
During my life thou shalt me not beguile.
Trust shall I God, to enter in awhile
His haven of heaven sure and uniform,
Ever after thy calm, look I for a storm.
Long was I, Lady Luck, your serving man,
And now have lost again all that I got,
Wherefore when I think on you now and then,
And in my mind remember this and that,
Ye may not blame me though I beshrew [1]
But in faith I bless you again a thousand times,
For lending me now some leisure [2]
To make rhymes.

1. Beshrew = to curse. 2. 'Beshrew' and 'leisure' rhymed in More's day.

Anonymous c1540

The Wreck of Walsingham

(Perhaps the most celebrated shrine of late mediæval England
was that of Our Lady at Walsingham in Norfolk. In 1538 the
shrine was wrecked by Cromwell's order. The portrait of
Mary was taken by cart from Walsingham to Chelsea, where
it was publicly burnt. The shrine was restored towards the
end of the nineteenth century.)

In the wrecks of Walsingham
Whom should I choose,
But the queen of Walsingham
To be guide to my muse?
Then, thou Prince of Walsingham,
Grant me to frame
Bitter plaints to rue thy wrong,
Bitter woe for thy name.

Bitter was it, oh, to see
The silly sheep

Murdered by the ravening wolves,
While the shepherds did sleep.
Bitter was it, oh, to view
The sacred vine,
While the gardeners played all close,
Rooted up by the swine.
Bitter, bitter, oh to behold
The grass to grow
Where the walls of Walsingham
So stately did show.

Such were the works of Walsingham,
While she did stand:
Such are the wrecks as now do show
Of that holy land.
Level, level with the ground
The towers do lie,
Which, with their golden glittering tops,
Pierced once to the sky.

Where were gates, no gates are now
The ways unknown
Where the press of peers did pass,
While her fame far was blown.
Owls do shriek, where the sweetest hymns
Lately were sung:
Toads and serpents hold their dens,
Where the palmers did throng.

Weep, weep, O Walsingham
Whose days are nights:
Blessings turned to blasphemies,
Holy deeds to despites;
Sin is where Our Lady sat;
Heaven turned is to hell:
Satan sits where Our Lord did sway –
Walsingham, oh farewell!

Anonymous c1540

On the Eve of Execution

O death, O death, rock me asleep,
Bring me to quiet rest,
Let pass my weary guiltless ghost
Out of my careful breast.
Toll on the passing bell,
Ring out my doleful knell,
Thy sound my death abroad will tell,
For I must die:
There is no remedy.

My pains, my pains, who can express?
Alas, they are so strong,
My dolours will not suffer strength
My life for to prolong
Toll on the passing bell,
Ring out my doleful knell,
Thy sound my death abroad will tell,
For I must die:
There is no remedy.

Alone, alone in prison strong,
I wail my destiny;
Woe worth this cruel hap, that I
Must taste this misery.
Toll on the passing bell,
Ring out my doleful knell,
Thy sound my death abroad will tell,
For I must die:
There is no remedy.

Farewell, farewell, my pleasures past,
Welcome my present pain:
I feel my torment so increase
That life cannot remain.

Cease now then, passing bell,
Ring out my doleful knell,
For thou my death doth tell;
Lord, pity thou my soul,
Death doth draw nigh;
Sound dolefully,
For now I die,
I die, I die.

Henry Howard, Earl of Surrey 1517-1547

A Portrait of Henry VIII

The Assyrian King in peace, with foul desire
And filthy lusts, that stained his regal heart
In war that should set princely hearts on fire:
Did yield, vanquished for want of martial art.
The dint of swords from kisses seemed strange
And harder, than his lady's side, his targe [1]
From glutton feasts, to soldier's fare a change.
His helmet, far above a garland's charge.
Who scarce the name of manhood did retain,
Drenched in sloth, and womanish delight,
Feeble of spirit, impatient of pain:
When he had lost his honour, and his right:
Proud, time of wealth, in storms appalled with dread,
Murdered himself to show some manful deed.

1. Targe = target.

St Philip Howard 1557-1595

Hymn

O Christ, the glorious Crown
Of virgins that are pure;
Who dost a love and thirst for Thee
Within their minds procure;
Thou art the spouse of those
That chaste and humble be,

The hope, the life, the only help
Of such as trust in Thee.

All charity of those
Whose souls Thy love doth warm;
All simple pleasures of such minds
As think no kind of harm;
All sweets delight wherewith
The patient hearts abound,
Do blaze Thy name, and with Thy praise
They make the world resound.

The sky, the land, the sea,
And all on earth below,
The glory of Thy worthy Name
Do with their praises show.
The winter yields Thee praise,
The summer doth the same,
The sun, the moon, the stars and all
Do magnify Thy name.

The roses that appear
So fair in outward sight;
The violets which with their scent
Do yield so great delight;
The pearls, the precious stones,
The birds, Thy praise do sing,
The woods, the wells, and all delights,
Which from this earth do spring.

What creature, O sweet Lord
From praising Thee can stay?
What earthly thing but, filled with joy,
Thine honour bewray?
Let us, therefore, with praise
Thy mighty works express,
With heart and hand, with mind, and all
Which we from Thee possess.

Chidiock Tichborne 1558-1586, martyr

Retrospect (written in prison)

My prime of youth is but a frost of cares,
My feast of joy is but a dish of pain,
My crop of corn is but a field of tares,
And all my good is but vain hope of gain.
The day is past and yet I saw no sun,
And now I live, and now my life is done.

The spring is past, and yet it hath not sprung;
The fruit is dead, and yet the leaves are green
My youth is gone, and yet I am but young;
I saw the world, and yet I was not seen
My thread is cut, and yet it is not spun,
And now I live, and now my life is done.

I sought my death, and found it in my womb;
I looked for life, and saw it was a shade
I trod the earth, and knew it was my tomb;
And now I die, and now I am but made.
The glass is full, and now my glass is run,
And now I live, and now my life is done.

St Henry Walpole SJ 1558-1595, martyr

Martyrdom of Fr Campion

England, look up! Thy soil is stained with blood,
Thou hast made martyrs many of thine own,
If thou hadst Grace, their deaths would do thee good.
The seed will take, which in such blood is sown,
And Campion's learning fertile so before,
Thus watered too, must needs of force be more.

All Europe wonders at so rare a man,
England is filled with rumour of his end.
London must needs, for it was present then

When constantly three saints their lives did spend,
The streets, the stones, the steps, they hale them by,
Proclaim the cause, for which these martyrs die.

The Tower says, the truth he did defend,
The Bar bears witness of his guiltless mind,
Tyburn doth tell, he made a patient end.
In every gate his martyrdom we find.
In vain you wrought, that would obscure his name,
For heaven and earth will still record the same.

His quartered limbs shall join with joy again,
And rise a body brighter than the sun,
Your bloody malice tormented him in vain,
For every wrench some glory hath him won.
And every drop of blood, which he did spend,
Hath reaped a joy, which never shall have end.

The Song of Mary the Mother of Christ

Fain would I write, my mind ashamed is,
My verse doth fear to do the matter wrong:
No earthly music good enough for this,
Not David's harp, nor Hierom's mourning song.
Nor Esaie's lips are worthy once to move,
Though Seraphim's fire hath kindled them with love.

Then sing, O saints, O holy heavenly choir!
And I shall strive to follow on your song:
This sacred ditty is my chief desire,
My soul to hear this music now doth long.
And longing thus, all wist, there was no din,
They silent stood, to see who should begin.

For none did think him worthy to be one,
And every one to other there gave place:
But bowing knees to Jesus every one,
They him besought for to decide the case.

Who said to me, most fit for this appears
My mother's plaint, and sacred virgin tears.

Straight all agreed. The Virgin ready pressed
To do the will of her eternal Son:
With heavenly cheer and most melodious breast
Her sacred song and ditty thus begun.
Bowing herself unto the glorious throne,
Where Three did sit adored all in one.

And still as they the Virgin singing hear,
In self same time, so echoed all the choir:
Thou only Son of God, Father of might,
Maker of me and all, the well of grace:
Fountain of love, eternal Son of light,
Became my Son; and falling on her face,
Repeating this full oft (with music sweet)
She did adore and kiss our Saviour's feet.

O how my cross was ever mixed with sweet!
My pain with joy, mine earth with heavenly bliss!
Who always might adore my Saviour's feet.
Embrace my God, my loving infant kiss.
And give Him suck, Who gives the angels meat.

St Robert Southwell SJ, 1561-1595, martyr

Mary Magdalen's Lament at Christ's Death

Sith my life from life is parted: [1]
Death come take thy portion,
Who survives, when life is murdered,
Lives by mere extortion. [2]
All that live, and not in God,
Couch their life in death's abode.

Seely stars must needs leave shining,[3]
When the sun is shadowed.
Borrowed streams refrain their running,
When head springs are hindered.
One that lives by others' breath,
Dyeth also by his death.

O true life, since thou hast left me,
Mortal life is tedious,
Death it is to live without thee,
Death of all most odious.
Turn again, or take me to thee,
Let me die or live thou in me.

Where the truth once was and is not,
Shadows are but vanity:
Showing want, that help they cannot,
Signs, not salves of misery.
Painted meats no hunger feeds,
Dying life each death exceeds.

With my love, my life was nestled
In the sum of happiness;
From my love, my life is wrested
To a world of heaviness.
O let love my life remove
Sith I live not where I love.

O my soul what did unloose thee
From thy sweet captivity?
God, not I, did still posses thee:
His, not mine thy liberty.
O too happy thrall thou wert,
When thy prison was his heart.

Spiteful spear, that break'st this prison,
Seat of all felicity,

Working this, with double treason,
Love's and life's delivery:
Through my life thou draw'st away,
Maugre thee my life shall stay. [4]

1. Sith = in truth. 2. Extortion = lives by exploiting the world. 3. Seely = holy, innocent. 4. Maugre = despite.

Fortune's Falsehood

In worldly merriments lurketh much misery,
Sly fortune's subtleties, in bait of happiness
Shroud hooks, that swallowed without recovery,
Murder the innocent with mortal heaviness.

She sootheth appetites with pleasing vanities,
Till they be conquered with cloaked tyranny;
Then changing countenance, with open enmities
She triumphs over them, scorning their slavery.

With fawning flattery death's door she openeth,
Alluring passengers to bloody destiny;
In offers bountiful, in proof she beggareth,
Men's ruins registering her false felicity.

Her hopes are fastened in bliss that vanisheth,
Her smart inherited with sure possession;
Constant in cruelty, she never altereth
But from one violence to more oppression.

To those that follow her, favours are measured,
As easy premisses to hard conclusions;
With bitter corrosives her joys are seasoned,
Her highest benefits are but illusions.

Of the Blessed Sacrament of the Altar – the Christian's Manna

In paschal feast, the end of ancient rite,
An entrance was to never-ending grace;

Types to the truth, dim glimpses to the light;
Performing deed presaging signs did chase:
Christ's final meal was fountain of our good,
For mortal meat He gave immortal food.

That which He gave, He was: O peerless gift!
Both God and man He was, and both He gave.
He in His hand Himself did truly lift,
Far off they see whom in themselves they have;
Twelve did He feed, twelve did their feeder eat,
He made, He dressed, He gave, He was their meat.

They saw, they heard, they felt Him sitting near,
Unseen, unfelt, unheard, they Him received;
No diverse thing, though diverse it appear;
Though senses fail, yet faith is not deceived;
And if the wonder of the work be new,
Believe the work because His word is true.

Here truth belief; as belief inviteth love,
So sweet a truth love never yet enjoyed;
What thought can think, what will doth best approve,
Is here obtained where no desire is void:
The grace, the joy, the treasure here is such,
No wit can wish, nor will embrace so much.

Self-love here cannot crave more than it finds;
Ambition to no higher worth aspire;
The eagerest famine of most hungry minds
May fill, yea far exceed their own desire:
In sum here is all in a sum expressed,
Of much the most, of every good the best.

To ravish eyes here heavenly beauties are;
To win the ear sweet music's sweetest sound;
To lure the taste the angel's heavenly fare;
To soothe the sent divine perfumes abound;

To please the touch, He in our hearts doth bed,
Whose touch doth cure the deaf, the dumb, the dead.

Here to delight the wit true wisdom is,
To woo the will – of every good the choice;
For memory, a mirror showing bliss;
Here's all that can both sense and soul rejoice;
And if to all, all this it do not bring,
The fault is in the men, not in the thing.

Though blind men see no light, the sun doth shine;
Sweet cakes are sweet, though fevered tastes deny it;
Pearls precious are, though trodden on by swine;
Each truth is true, though all men do not try it;
The best still to the bad doth work the worst;
Things bred to bliss do make them more accursed.

The angels' eyes, whom veils cannot deceive,
Might best disclose that best they do discern;
Men must with sound and silent faith receive
More than they can by sense or reason learn;
God's power our proofs, His works our wit exceed,
The doer's might is reason of His deed.

A body is endowed with ghostly rights;
And Nature's work from Nature's law is free;
In heavenly sun lie hid eternal lights,
Lights clear and near, yet them no eye can see.
Dead forms a never-dying life do shroud;
A boundless sea lies in a little cloud.

The God of Hosts in slender host doth dwell,
Yea, God and man with all to either due,
That God that rules the heavens and rifled hell,
That man whose death did us to life renew:
That God and man that is the angels' bliss,
In form of bread and wine our nurture is.

Whole may His body be in smallest bread,
Whole in the whole, yea whole in every crumb;
With which be one or be ten thousand fed,
All to each one, to all but one doth come,
And though each one as much as all receive,
Not one too much, nor all too little have.

One soul in man is all in every part;
One face at once in many mirrors shines;
One fearful noise doth make a thousand start;
One eye at once of countless things defines;
If proofs of one in many Nature frame,
God may in stranger sort perform the same.

God present is at once in every place,
Yet God in every place is ever one;
So may there be by gifts of ghostly grace,
One man in many rooms, yet filling none;
Since angels may effects of bodies shew,
God angels' gifts on bodies may bestow.

What God as author made He alter may,
No change so hard as making all of naught;
If Adam framed was of slimy clay,
Bread may to Christ's most sacred flesh be wrought.
He may do this that made with mighty hand
Of water wine, a snake of Moses' wand.

A Preparation to Prayer

When thou dost talk with God, by prayer I mean,
Lift up pure hands, lay down all lust's desires:
Fix thoughts on heaven, present a conscience clean:
Such holy balm, to mercy's throne aspires.
Confess fault's guilt, crave pardon for thy sin;
Tread holy paths, call grace to guide therein.

It is the spirit with reverence must obey
Our Maker's will, to practice what He taught;
Make not the flesh thy counsel when thou pray:
'Tis enemy to every virtuous thought:
It is the foe we daily feed and clothe:
It is the prison that the soul doth loathe.

Even as Elias, mounting to the sky,
Did cast his mantle to the Earth behind:
So, when the heart presents the prayer on high,
Exclude the world from traffic with the mind.
Lips near to God, and ranging hearts within,
Is but vain babbling and converts to sin.

Like Abraham, ascending up the hill,
To sacrifice; his servants left below,
That he might act the great Commander's will,
Without impeach to his obedient blow;
Even so the soul, remote from earthly things;
Should mount salvation's shelter, Mercy's wings.

Examples of Our Saviour

Our Saviour, (pattern of true holiness),
Continual prayed, us by example teaching,
When He was baptised in the wilderness,
In working miracles and in His preaching;
Upon the mount, in garden-groves of death,
At His Last Supper, at His parting breath.

Oh! Fortress of the faithful, sure defence,
In which doth Christians' cognizance consist;
Their victory, their triumph comes from thence,
So forcible, hell-gates cannot resist:
A thing whereby both angels, clouds, and stars,
At man's request fight God's revengeful wars.

Nothing more grateful in the Highest eyes,
Nothing more firm in danger to protect us,
Nothing more forcible to pierce the skies,
And not depart 'til Mercy do respect us:
And, as the soul life to the body gives,
So prayer revives the soul, by prayer it lives.

Look Home

Retired thoughts enjoy their own delights,
As beauty doth, in self-beholding eye;
Man's mind a mirror is, of heavenly sights,
A brief, wherein all marvels summed lie;
Of fairest forms and sweetest shapes the store,
Most graceful all, yet thought may grace them more.

The mind a creature is, yet can create,
To nature's patterns adding higher skill;
Of finest works, wit better could the state
If force of wit had equal power of will;
Devise of man in working hath no end;
What thought can think, another thought can mend.

Man's soul, of endless beauties image is,
Drawn by the work of endless skill and might;
This skilful might gave many sparks of bliss,
And to discern this bliss a native light.
To flame God's image as his worths required,
His might, his skill, his word, and will conspired.

All that he had, his image should present;
All that it should present, he could afford;
To that he could afford, his will was bent,
His will was followed with performing word.
Let this suffice, by this conceive the rest:
He should, he could, he would, he did the best.

The Nativity of Christ

Behold the father is his daughter's son,
The bird that built the nest is hatched therein,
The old of years an hour hath not outrun,
Eternal life to live doth now begin,
The Word is dumb, the mirth of heaven doth weep,
Might feeble is, and force doth faintly creep.

O dying souls, behold your living spring;
O dazzled eyes, behold your sun of grace;
Dull ears, attend what word this Word doth bring;
Up, heavy hearts, with joy your joy embrace.
From death, from dark, from deafness, from despairs,
This life, this light, this Word, this joy repairs.

Gift better than Himself God doth not know;
Gift better than His God no man can see.
This gift doth here the giver given bestow;
Gift to this gift let each receiver be.
God is my gift, Himself he freely gave me;
God's gift am I, and none but God shall have me.

Man altered was by sin from man to beast;
Beast's food is hay, hay is all mortal flesh.
Now God is flesh and lies in manger pressed
As hay, the brutest sinner to refresh.
O happy field wherein this fodder grew,
Whose taste doth us from beasts to men renew.

The Burning Babe

As I in hoary winter's night stood shivering in the snow,
Surprised I was with sudden heat which made my heart
    to glow;
And lifting up a fearful eye to view what fire was near,
A pretty Babe all burning bright did in the air appear;

Who scorched with excessive heat, such floods of tears
  did shed,
As though his floods should quench his flames which with
  his tears were fed.

'Alas!' quoth he, 'but newly born in fiery heats I fry,
Yet none approach to warm their hearts or feel my fire but I.
My faultless breast the furnace is, the fuel wounding thorns;
Love is the fire, and sighs the smoke, the ashes shame
  and scorns;
The fuel justice layeth on, and mercy blows the coals;
The metal in this furnace wrought are men's defiled souls:
For which, as now on fire I am to work them to their good,
So will I melt into a bath to wash them in my blood.'
With this he vanished out of sight and swiftly shrunk away,
And straight I called unto mind that it was Christmas day.

Lewd Love is Loss

Misdeeming eye! That stoopest to the lure
Of mortal worths, not worth so worthy love;
All beauty's base, all graces are impure
That do thy erring thoughts from God remove.
Sparks to the fire, the beams yield to the Sun,
All grace to God, from whom all graces run.

If picture more, more should the pattern please;
No shadow can with shadowed thing compare;
And fairest shapes, whereon our loves do cease,
But seely signs of God's high beauties are.[1]
Go, starving sense, feed thou on earthly mast;[2]
True love, in heaven seek thou thy sweet repast.

Glean not in barren soil these offal-ears,
Sith reap thou mayst whole heavens of delight;
Base joys with griefs, bad hopes do end in fears,
Lewd love with loss, evil peace with deadly fight:

God's love alone doth end with endless ease,
Whose joys in hope, whose hope concludes in peace.

Let not the luring train of fancies trap,
Or gracious features, proofs of Nature's skill,
Lull Reason's force asleep in Error's lap,
Or draw thy wit to bent of wanton will.
The fairest flowers have not the sweetest smell,
A seeming Heaven proves oft a damning Hell.

Self-pleasing souls that play with Beauty's bait
In shining shroud may swallow fatal hook;
Where eager sight on semblant fair doth wait
A lock it proves that first was but a look!
The fish with ease into the net doth glide,
But to get out the way is not so wide.

So long the fly doth dally with the flame
Until his singed wings do force his fall;
So long the eye doth follow fancy's game
Till Love hath left the heart in heavy thrall.
Soon may the mind be cast in Cupid's gale,
But hard it is imprisoned thoughts to bail.

O loathe that Love whose final aim is lust,
Moth of the mind, eclipse of Reason's light
The grave of Grace, the mole of Nature's rust,[3]
The wreck of Wit, the wrong of every Right.
In sum, an evil whose harms no tongue can tell;
In which to live is death, to die is Hell.

Seely = holy. 2. Mast = pigswill. 3. Mole: here in anatomical sense.

Life is but Loss (written in the Tower)

By force I live, in will I wish to die
In plaint I pass the length of lingering days;
Free would my soul from mortal body fly,

And tread the track of death's desired ways:
Life is but loss where death is deemed gain,
And loathed pleasures breed displeasing pain.

Who would not die to kill all murdering grieves? [1]
Or who would live in never-dying fears?
Who would not wish his treasure safe from thieves
And quit his heart from pangs, his eyes from tears?
Death parteth but two ever-fighting foes,
Whose civil strife doth work our endless woes.

Life is a wandering course to doubtful rest;
As oft a cursed rise to damning leap,
As happy race to win a heavenly crest;
None being sure what final fruits to reap:
And who can like in such a life to dwell,
Whose ways are strait to Heaven but wide to Hell?

Come, cruel death, why lingerest thou so long?
What doth withhold thy dint from fatal stroke? [2]
Now pressed I am, alas! Thou dost me wrong
To let me live more anger to provoke:
Thy right is had when thou has stopped my breath
Why shouldst thou stay to work my double death?

If Saul's attempt in falling on his blade
As lawful were as eth[3] to put in ure, [4]
If Sampson's leave a common law were made,
Of Abels' lot, if all that were sure,
Then, cruel Death, thou should'st the tyrant play
With none but such as wished for delay.

Where life is loved thou ready are to kill,
And to abridge with sudden pangs their joy;
Where life is loathed thou wilt not work their joy;
But dost adjourn their death to their annoy.
To some thou art a fierce unbidden guest,
But those that crave thy help thou helpest least.

Avaunt, O viper! I thy spite defy:
There is a God that over-rules thy force,
Who can thy weapons to His will apply,
And shorten or prolong our brittle course.
I on His mercy not thy might rely,
To Him I live, for Him I hope to die.

1. grieves = griefs. 2. Dint = attack. 3. Eth = easy. 4. Ure = use.

Henry Constable 1562-1613

Love's Franciscan

Sweet hand! The sweet yet cruel bow thou art,
From whence at one, five ivory arrows fly,
So with five wounds at once I wounded lie
Bearing in breast the print of every dart.
St Francis had the like, yet felt no smart
Where I in living torments never die,
His wounds were in his hands and feet, where I
All these same helpless wounds feel in my heart.
Now as St Francis (if a saint) am I.
The bow which shot these shafts a relic is
I mean the hand, which is the reason why
So many for devotion thee would kiss,
And I thy glove kiss as a thing divine;
Thy arrows quiver, and thy relics shine.

To the Blessed Sacrament

When Thee (O holy sacrificed Lamb)
 In severed signs I white and liquid see,
As in Thy body slain I think on Thee,
Which pale by shedding of Thy blood became.
And when again I do behold the same
Veiled in white to be received of me,
Thou seemest in thy sindon wrapt to be [1]
Like to a corse, whose monument I am. [2]

115

Buried in me, unto my soul appear,
Prisoned in earth, and banished from Thy sight,
Like our forefathers who in Limbo were,
Clear thou my thoughts, as thou didst give them light,
And as thou others freed from purging fire
Quench in my heart the flames of bad desire.

1. Sindon = shroud. 2. Corse = corpse.

To Our Blessed Lady

In that (O Queen of Queens) thy birth was free
From guilt, which others do of grace bereave,
When in their mother's womb they life receive
As His sole-borne daughter loved thee.
To match thee like thy birth's nobility,
He thee His Spirit for thy spouse did leave
Of whom thou didst His only Son conceive,
And so wast linked to all the Trinity.
Cease then, O queens who earthly crowns do wear,
To glory in the pomp of worldly things;
If men such high respect unto you bear
Which daughters, wives, and mothers are of kings,
What honour should unto that Queen be done
Who had your God for Father, Spouse and Son!

William Shakespeare 1564-1616

Purgatory – (The Ghost Speaks: Hamlet, *Act I, scene 5)*

'I am thy father's spirit,
Doomed for a certain term to walk the night,
And for the day confined to fast in fires,
'Til the foul crimes done in my days of nature
Are burnt and purged away. But that I am forbid
To tell the secrets of my prison-house,
I could a tale unfold whose lightest word
Would harrow up thy soul, freeze thy young blood,
Make thy two eyes, like stars, start from their spheres,

Thy knotted and combined locks to part,
And each particular hair to stand on end,
Like quills upon the fretful porcupine;
But this eternal blazon must not be
To ears of flesh and blood...
...Sleeping within my orchard,
My custom always of the afternoon,
Upon my secure hour thy uncle stole,
With juice of cursed hebanon in a vial,
And in the porches of my ears did pour
The leprous distilment; whose effect
Holds such an enmity with blood of man
That swift as quicksilver it courses through
The natural gates and alleys of the body,
And with a sudden vigour it doth posset
And curd, like eager droppings into milk,
The thin and wholesome blood; so did it mine;
And a most instant tetter barked about, [1]
Most lazar like, with vile and loathsome crust, [2]
All my smooth body.
Thus was I, sleeping, by a brother's hand,
Of life, of crown, of queen, at once dispatched:
Cut off even in the blossoms of my sin,
Unhouseled,[3] disappointed, unannealed,[4]
No reckoning made, but sent to my account
With all my imperfections on my head:
O, horrible! O, horrible! Most horrible!'

1.Tetter = skin-rash. 2. Lazar = like a leper. 3. Unhouseled = without receiving communion. 4. Unannealed = not strengthened by receiving the Last Rites.

The Good Friar (Romeo and Juliet – Act II, scene 2)

Romeo:
'Hence will I to my ghostly father's cell, [1]
His help to crave, and my dear hap to tell.'

SCENE III. Friar Laurence's cell.
Enter Friar Laurence with a basket.

Friar Laurence:
'The grey-eyed morn smiles on the frowning night,
Chequering the eastern clouds with streaks of light,
And flecked darkness like a drunkard reels
From forth day's path and Titan's fiery wheels.
Now, ere the suit advance his burning eye,
The day to cheer and night's dank dew to dry,
I must up-fill this osier cage of ours
With baleful weeds and precious-juiced flowers.
The earth that's nature's mother is her tomb;
What is her burying grave that is her womb,
And from her womb children of divers kind
We sucking on her natural bosom find,
Many for many virtues excellent,
None but for some and yet all different.
O, mickle is the powerful grace that lies [2]
In herbs, plants, stones, and their true qualities
For nought so vile that on the earth doth live
But to the earth some special good doth give,
Nor aught so good but strained from that fair use
Revolts from true birth, stumbling on abuse:
Virtue itself turns vice, being misapplied;
And vice sometimes by action dignified.
Within the infant rind of this small flower
Poison hath residence and medicine power:
For this, being smelt, with that part cheers each part;
Being tasted, slays all senses with the heart.
Two such opposed kings encamp them still
In man as well as herbs, grace and rude will;

And where the worser is predominant,
Full soon the canker death eats up that plant.'

Sonnet 73

That time of year thou mayst in me behold
When yellow leaves, or none, or few, do hang
Upon those boughs which shake against the cold,
Bare ruined choirs, where late the sweet birds sang.
In me thou see'st the twilight of such day
As after sunset fadeth in the west;
Which by and by black night doth take away,
Death's second self, that seals up all in rest.
In me thou see'st the glowing of such fire,
That on the ashes of his youth doth lie,
As the death-bed whereon it must expire,
Consumed with that which it was nourished by.
This thou perceivest, which makes thy love more strong
To love that well which thou must leave ere long.

Sonnet 94

They that have power to hurt and will do none,
That do not do the thing they most do show,
Who, moving others, are themselves as stone,
Unmoved, cold, and to temptation slow;
They rightly do inherit heaven's graces,
And husband nature's riches from expense;
They are the lords and owners of their faces,
Others but stewards of their excellence.
The summer's flower is to the summer sweet,
Though to itself it only live and die,
But if that flower with base infection meet,
The basest weed outbraves his dignity:
For sweetest things turn sourest by their deeds;
Lilies that fester smell far worse than weeds.

Sonnet 121

'Tis better to be vile than vile esteemed,
When not to be receives reproach of being;
And the just pleasure lost, which is so deemed
Not by our feeling, but by others' seeing:
For why should others' false adulterate eyes
Give salutation to my sportive blood?
Or on my frailties why are frailer spies,
Which in their wills count bad what I think good?
No, I am that I am, and they that level
At my abuses reckon up their own:
I may be straight though they themselves be bevel;
By their rank thoughts my deeds must not be shown;
Unless this general evil they maintain,
All men are bad and in their badness reign.

Sonnet 129

The expense of spirit in a waste of shame
Is lust in action; and till action, lust
Is perjured, murderous, bloody, full of blame,
Savage, extreme, rude, cruel, not to trust;
Enjoyed no sooner but despised straight;
Past reason hunted; and no sooner had,
Past reason hated, as a swallowed bait,
On purpose laid to make the taker mad:
Mad in pursuit, and in possession so;
Had, having, and in quest to have, extreme;
A bliss in proof, and proved, a very woe;
Before, a joy proposed; behind, a dream.
All this the world well knows; yet none knows well
To shun the heaven that leads men to this hell.

Sonnet 146

Poor soul, the centre of my sinful earth,
Thrall to these rebel powers that thee array,
Why dost thou pine within and suffer dearth,

Painting thy outward walls so costly gay?
Why so large cost, having so short a lease,
Dost thou upon thy fading mansion spend?
Shall worms, inheritors of this excess,
Eat up thy charge? Is this thy body's end?
Then, soul, live thou upon thy servant's loss,
And let that pine to aggravate thy store;
Buy terms divine in selling hours of dross;
Within be fed, without be rich no more:
So shalt thou feed on Death, that feeds on men,
And Death once dead, there's no more dying then.

Fr Henry Fitzsimmon SJ 1566-1643

On Oaths

In elder times an ancient custom 'twas,
To swear in weighty matters by the Mass.
But when Mass was put down, as old men note,
They swore then by the Cross of this grey groat.
And when the Cross was held likewise in scorn
Then Faith and Truth, for common oaths were sworn.
But now men banished have both Faith and Truth,
So that 'God damn me', is the common oath.
So custom keeps Decorum, by gradation,
Losing Mass, Cross, Faith, Truth – followeth damnation.

William Alabaster 1567-1640

Upon the Signs of Christ's Crucifying

O sweet and bitter monuments of pain,
Bitter to Christ who all pain endured,
But sweet to me, whose death my life procured;
How shall I full express such loss, such gain?
My tongue shall be my pen, mine eyes shall rain
Tears for my ink, the Cross where I was cured
Shall be my book, where having all abjured
And calling heavens to record in that plain

Thus plainly will I write: *no sin like mine.*
When I have done, do Thou Jesu divine
Take up the tart sponge of Thy Passion
And blot it forth: then be Thy spirit the Quill,
Thy blood the Ink, and with compassion
Write upon my soul: *thy Jesu still.*

Incarnatio est Maximum Dei Donum (The Incarnation is the Greatest Gift of God)

Like as the fountain of all light created
Doth power out streams of brightness undefined
Through all the conduits of transparent kind
That heaven and air are both illuminated,
And yet his light is not thereby abated;
So God's eternal bounty ever shined
The beams of being, moving, life, sense, mind,
And to all things Himself communicated.
But see the violent diffusive pleasure
Of goodness, that left not, till God had spent
Himself by giving us Himself His treasure
In making man a God omnipotent.
How might this goodness draw our souls above
Which drew down God with such attractive Love.

Ben Jonson 1572-1637

To Heaven

Good and great God, can I not think of Thee
But it must, straight, my melancholy be?
Is it interpreted in me disease
That, laden with my sins, I seek for ease?
O be Thou witness, that the reins dost know [1]
And hearts of all, if I be sad for show,
And judge me after, if I dare pretend
To aught but grace, or aim at other end.
As Thou art all, so be Thou all to me,
First, midst, and last, converted, one and three;

My faith, my hope, my love; and in this state
My judge, my witness, and my advocate.
Where have I been this while exiled from Thee,
And whither rapped, now Thou but stoop'st to me?
Dwell, dwell here still. O, being everywhere,
How can I doubt to find Thee ever, here?
I know my state, both full of shame and scorn,
Conceived in sin, and unto labour born,
Standing with fear, and must with horror fall,
And destined unto judgement, after all.
I feel my griefs too, and there scarce is ground
Upon my flesh to inflict another wound.
Yet dare I not complain, or wish for death
With holy PAUL, lest it be thought the breath
Of discontent; or that these prayers be
For weariness of life, not love of Thee.

1. Reins, here = loins.

A Hymn on the Nativity

I sing the birth was born to-night,
The Author both of Life and Light;
The Angel so did sound it,
And like the ravished shepherds said,
Who saw the light, and were afraid,
Yet searched, and true they found it.

The Son of God, the Eternal King,
That did us all salvation bring,
And freed the soul from danger;
He whom the whole world could not take,
The Word, which Heaven and Earth did make,
Was now laid in a manger.

The Father's wisdom willed it so,
The Son's obedience knew no No.
Both wills were in one stature,
And as that wisdom had decreed,

The Word was now made Flesh indeed,
And took on Him our nature.

What comfort by Him do we win,
Who made Himself the price of sin
To make us heirs of glory?
To see this Babe all innocence,
A Martyr born in our defence:
Can man forget this story?

A Hymn to God the Father

Hear me, O God!
A broken heart,
Is my best part:
Use still thy rod
That I may prove
Therein, thy Love.

If thou hadst not
Been stern to me,
But left me free,
I had forgot
My self and thee.

For, sin's so sweet,
As minds ill bent
Rarely repent,
Until they meet
Their punishment.

Who more can crave
Than thou hast done?
That gav'st a Son,
To free a slave,
First made of nought;
With all since bought.

Sin, Death and Hell,
His glorious Name
Quite overcame,
Yet I rebel,
And slight the same.

But, I'll come in,
Before my loss
Me farther toss,
As sure to win
Under His Cross.

The Garland of the Blessed Virgin Marie

Here, are five letters in this blessed Name,
Which, changed, a five-fold mystery design,
The *M*. the *M*yrtle, *A*. the *A*lmonds claim,
R. *R*ose, *I*. *I*vy, *E*. sweet *E*glantine.

These form thy Garland. Whereof *Myrtle* green,
The gladdest ground to all the numbered-five,
Is so implexed, and laid in, between,
As Love, here studied to keep Grace alive.

The second string is the sweet *Almond* bloom
Amounted high upon *Selinis* crest:
As it, alone, (and only it) had room,
To knit thy Crown, and glorify the rest.

The third, is from the garden called the *Rose,*
The Eye of flowers, worthy, for his scent,
To top the fairest Lilly, now, that grows,
With wonder on the thorny regiment.

The fourth is humble *Ivy,* insert,
But lowly laid, as on the earth asleep.
Preserved, in her antique bed of *Vert,*
No faith's more firm, or flat, then, where't doth creep.

But, that which sums all, is the *Eglantine,*
Which, of the field is cleped the sweetest brier, [1]
Inflamed with ardour to that mystic shine,
In *Moses'* bush, un-wasted in the fire.

Thus, Love, and Hope, and burning Charity,
(Divinest graces) are so intermixed,
With odorous sweets, and soft humility,
As if they adored the Head, whereon th'are fixed.

These Mysteries do point to three more great,
On the reverse of this your circling crown,
All, pouring their full shower of graces down,
The glorious *Trinity* in *Union* met.

Daughter, and Mother, and the Spouse of God,
Alike of kin, to that most blessed *Trine,*
Of Persons, yet in Union (One) divine.
How are thy gifts, and graces blazed abroad!

Most holy, and pure Virgin, blessed Maid,
Sweet Tree of Life, King *David's* Strength and Tower,
The House of Gold, the Gate of Heaven's power,
The Morning-star, whose light our Fall hath stayed.

Great Queen of Queens, most mild, most meek, most wise,
Most venerable. Cause of all our joy.
Whose cheerful look our sadness doth destroy,
And art the spotless Mirror to Man's eyes.

The Seat of Sapience, the most lovely Mother,
And most to be admired of thy Sex,
Who mad'st us happy all, in thy reflex,
By bringing forth God's only Son, no other.

Thou Throne of glory, beauteous as the Moon,
The rosy Morning, or the rising Sun,

Who like a Giant hastes his course to run,
Till he hath reached his two-fold point of Noon.

How are thy gifts and graces blazed abroad,
Through all the lines of this circumference,
Th' imprint in all purged hearts this virgin sense,
Of being Daughter, Mother, Spouse of God?

1. Cleped (archaic) = called.

Fr John Thewlis c1580-1616, martyr

The Song of a Happy Rising

True Christian hearts cease to lament,
For grief it is in vain,
For Christ you know was well content
To suffer bitter pain
That we may come to Heaven's bliss,
There joyfully to sing.
Who doth believe shall never miss
To have a joyful rising!

But, England, here my heart is sad
For thy great cruelty
And loss of faith which once thou had
Of Christianity.
In thee false doctrine doth appear
Abundantly to spring,
Which is the cause, I greatly fear,
Thou lose thy happy rising!

As for myself, I am not afraid
To suffer constantly.
For why? Due debt must need be paid
Unto sweet God on high.
Saint Paul, he being firm of faith,
Hoping with saints to sing,

Most patiently did suffer death,
Lord, send us happy rising!

Mark well my ghostly victory,
My friends both great and small;
Be of firm faith, remember me
And dread not of your fall;
For you my sheep I shepherd have
Made labour for to bring
You to my fold, your souls to save.
Christ, send us happy rising!

I have said Mass and Matins both
And true Instructions taught,
Confirmed by the Holy Ghost
And mighty power wrought;
The Holy Communion also
With manna ever living,
The Holy Sacraments I taught.
Lord, send us happy rising!

Christ's passion oft before your face
I have declared plain,
How for our sins he suffered death
And how he rose again;
And how the twelve Apostles eke
Were put to death for preaching
The Catholic faith which Christ did teach.
Christ, send us happy rising!

The saints also did suffer death,
And martyrs, as you hear,
And I myself am now at hand,
But death I do not fear.
Then have I trust of greater grace
Unto my soul will bring,
When we shall meet both face to face
Before One heavenly King.

No hurdle hard nor hempen rope
Can make me once afraid,
No tyrant's knife against my life
Shall make me dismayed.
Though flesh and bones be broken and torn,
My soul I trust will sing
Amongst the glorious company
With Christ our heavenly King.

Thus I your friend John Thewlis
Have made my latest end,
Desiring God when his will is
Us all to heaven send,
Where neither strange nor damned crew
Can grief unto us bring,
And now I bid my last adieu.
Christ, send us happy rising!

Sir John Beaumont 1583-1627

On the Death of His Son

Dear Lord, receive my son, whose winning love
To me was like a friendship, far above
The course of nature or his tender age;
Whose looks could all my bitter griefs assuage:
Let his pure soul, ordained seven years to be
In that frail body which was a part of me,
Remain my pledge in Heaven, as sent to show
How to this port, at every step I go.

The Assumption

Who is she that ascends so high,
Next, the Heavenly King,
And about whom Angels fly
And her praises sing

Who is she that, adorned with light,
Makes the sun her robe,
At whose feet the queen of night
Lays her changing globe

To that crown direct thine eye,
Which her head attires
There thou mayst her name descry
Writ in starry fires.

This is she in whose pure womb
Heaven's Prince remained
Therefore in no earthly tomb
Can she be contained.

Heaven she was, which held that fire,
Whence the world took light,
And that Heaven doth now aspire
Flames with flames t' unite.

She that did so clearly shine
When our day begun,
See how bright her beams decline
Now she sits with the Sun.

Francis Beaumont 1584-1616

On the Tombs in Westminster Abbey

Mortality, behold and fear!
What a change of flesh, is here!
Think how many royal bones
Sleep within this heap of stones:
Here they lie had realms and lands,
Who now want strength to stir their hands:
Where from pulpits sealed with dust
They preach, 'In greatness is no trust.'
Here's an acre sown indeed

With the richest, royallest seed
That the earth did e'er suck in
Since the first man died for sin:
Here the bones of birth have cried –
'Though gods they were, as men they died.'
Here are sands, ignoble things,
Dropped from the ruined sides of kings;
Here's a world of pomp and state,
Buried in dust, once dead by fate.

Anonymous c1602

A Song of Four Priests who Suffered Death at Lancaster [1]

On this our English coast much blessed blood is shed,
Two hundred priests almost in our time martyred;
Many a layman die with joyful sufferance,
Many more in prison lie, God's cause for to advance.

Amongst this gracious troop that follow Christ his train,
To cause the Devil stoop four priests were lately slain;
Nutter's bold constancy with his sweet fellow Thwinge,
Of whose most meek modesty Angels and saints may sing.

Hunt's haughty courage stout with godly zeal so true
Mild Middleton, O what tongue can half thy virtue show?
At Lancaster lovingly these martyrs took their end
In glorious victory, true faith for to defend.

And thus Lancashire offered her sacrifice
To daunt their lewd desire, and please our Saviour's eyes,
For by this means I trust truth shall have victory
When as that number just of such saints complete be.

Who the Holy Ghost doth move unto his deity
In fervent flames of love thus sacrificed to be,
Whose faith and fortitude, whose grace and constancy
With mildness meek indeed confoundeth heresy.

131

Whose sacred members rent and quarters set on high [2]
Caused more to be content in the same cause to die,
Whose lives while they did live, whose blessed deaths also
Do admonition give what way we ought to go.

If we should them despise as many wretches do,
We should contemn likewise Our Blessed Saviour too.
Let their examples then move our hearts to relent
These were most blessed men whom God to us hath sent.

God's holy truth they taught and sealed it with their blood,
Dying with torments fraught and all to do us good,
Let lying heresy with her false libels lout, [3]
Truth will have victory, through such mild champions
    stout.

Praise be to God's good will, who doth his truth defend;
Lord, to thy vineyard still such worthy workmen send,
And, Good Lord, grant us grace that we may constant be.
With our Cross in each place to please Thy majesty.

1. Fr Robert Nutter and Fr Edward Twinge were martyred in 1600;
Fr Thurstan Hunt and Fr Robert Middleton accepted the same fate in 1601.
2. Catholic priests received the death penalty for high treason: hanging, drawing
and quartering, so that that their quartered limbs were put on show.
3. Lout = pay homage to.

PART III

Years of Endurance
1625-1744

By the time of the accession of King Charles I in 1625 the Church of England had become firmly established. The prospects of restoring the Catholic Church appeared remote, and Catholics became an increasingly small proportion of the population. It was a period of quiet endurance. Nevertheless, the two greatest poets of the late seventeenth century were Catholics: Dryden by conversion, Pope through birth.

James Shirley 1596-1666

A Dirge (from the play *Ajax and Ulysses*)

The glories of our blood and state
Are shadows, not substantial things;
There is no armour against Fate;
Death lays his icy hand on kings:
Sceptre and crown
Must tumble down,
And in the dust be equal made
With the poor crooked scythe and spade.

Some men with swords may reap the field,
And plant fresh laurels where they kill;
But their strong nerves at last must yield;
They tame but one another still:
Early or late
They stoop to fate,
And must give up their murmuring breath,
When they, poor captives, creep to death.

The garlands wither on your brow,
Then boast no more your mighty deeds!
Upon Death's purple altar now
See, where the victor-victim bleeds:
Your heads must come
To the cold tomb,
Only the actions of the just
Smell sweet and blossom in the dust.

A Bard Prophesies St Patrick's Coming to Ireland

A man shall come into this land
With shaven crown, and in his hand
A crooked staff; he shall command
And in the East his table stand:
From his warm lips a stream shall flow
To make rocks melt and churches grow.

Patrick Carey 1600-1650

Triolet

Yes, my dear Lord, I've found it so,
No joys but Thine are purely sweet;
Other delights come mixed with woe,
Yes, my dear Lord, I've found it so.
Pleasure at courts is but in show,
With true content in cells we meet;
Yes, my dear Lord, I've found it so,
No joys but Thine are purely sweet.

William Habington 1605-1654

Against Them Who Lay Unchastity to the Sex of Women [1]

They meet but with unwholesome springs,
And summers infectious are:
They hear but when the mermaid sings,
And only see the falling star:
Who ever dare,
Affirm no women chaste and fair.

Go cure your fevers: and you'll say
The dog-days scorch not all the year:
In copper mines no longer stay
But travel to the West, and there
The right ones see:
And grant all gold's not alchemy.

What madman 'cause the glow-worms flame
Is cold, swears there's no warmth in fire?
'Cause some make forfeit of their name,
And slave themselves to man's desire;
Shall the sex free
From guilt, dammed to bondage be?

Nor grieve, *Castara*, though 'twere frail,[2]
Thy virtue then would brighter shine,
When thy example should prevail,
And every woman's faith be thine,
And were there none;
'Tis majesty to rule alone.

1. This poem is a rebutal to Donne's 'Go, and Catch a Falling Star'.
2. Castara: a volume of poems dedicated to his future wife, Lucy Herbert.

Domine, Labia Mea Aperies (Open My Lips, O Lord)

No monument of me remain,
My memory rust
In the same marble with my dust,
Ere I the spreading laurel gain,
By writing wanton or profane.

Ye glorious wonders of the skies,
Shine still, bright stars,
The Almighty's mystic characters;
I'll not your beauteous lights surprise,
To illuminate a woman's eyes.

Nor, to perfume her veins, will I
In each one set
The purple of the violet:
The untouched flower may grow and die
Safe from my fancy's injury.

Open my lips, great God, and then
I'll soar above
The humble flight of carnal love.
Upward to Thee I'll force my pen,
And trace no path of vulgar men.

Quoniam Ego in Flagella Paratus Sum (Because I am Prepared to be Whipped)

Eternity, when I think thee;
(Which never any end must have,
Nor knewest beginning) and foresee
Hell is designed for sin a grave.

My frighted flesh trembles to dust,
My blood ebbs fearfully away:
Both guilty that they did to lust
And vanity my youth betray.

My eyes which from each beauteous sight
Drew spider-like black venom in,
Close like the marigold at night,
Oppressed with dew to bathe my sin.

My ears shut up that easy door
Which did proud fallacies admit,
And vow to hear no follies more,
Deaf to the charms of sin and wit.

My hands (which when they touched some fair
Imagined such an excellence,
As th'ermine's skin ungentle were)
Contract themselves and loose all sense.

No sorrow then shall enter in
With pity the great Judge's ears.
This moment's ours. Once dead, his sin
Men cannot expiate with tears.

The Reward of Innocent Love

We saw and wooed each other's eyes,
My soul contracted then with thine
And both burnt in one sacrifice;
By which our marriage grew divine.

137

Let wilder youths, whose soul is sense,
Profane the temple of delight,
And purchase endless penitence;
With the stolen pleasure of one night.

Time's ever ours, while we despise
The sensual idol of our clay,
For though the sun do set and rise;
We joy one everlasting day.

Whose light no jealous clouds obscure,
While each of us shines innocent.
The troubled stream is still impure:
With virtue flies away content.

And though opinion often err,
We'll court the modest smile of fame,
For sin's black danger circles her;
Who hath infection in her name.

Thus when to one dark silent room
Death shall our loving coffins thrust,
Fame will build columns on our tomb,
And add a perfume to our dust.

Sir William Davenant 1606-1668

Praise and Prayer

Praise is devotion for mighty minds,
The differing world's agreeing sacrifice;
Where Heaven divided faith united finds:
But prayer in various discord upward flies.

For prayer the ocean is where diversely
Men steer their course, each to a several coast;
Where all our interests so discordant be
That half begs winds by which the rest are lost.

By penitence when we ourselves forsake,
'Tis but in wise design on piteous Heaven;
In praise we nobly give what God may take,
And are, without a beggar's blush, forgiven.

Richard Crashaw 1612-1649

A Song of Divine Love

Lord, when the sense of Thy sweet grace
Sends up my soul to seek Thy face,
Thy blessed eyes breed such desire
I die in love's delicious fire.
O love, I am Thy sacrifice.
Be still triumphant, blessed eyes.
Still shine on me, fair suns, that I
Still may behold though still I die.

Though still I die, I live again,
Still longing so to be still slain;
So gainful is such loss of breath,
I die even in desire of death.
Still live in me this loving strife
Of living death and dying life:
For while Thou sweetly slayest me,
Dead to myself, I live in Thee.

Charitas Nimia: or the Dear Bargain

Lord, what is man?
Why should he cost Thee so dear?
What had his ruin lost Thee?
Lord, what is man that
Thou hast overbought
So much a thing of nought?
Love is too kind, I see, and can
Make but a simple merchantman;
'Twas for such sorry merchandise
Bold painters have put out his eyes.

Alas, sweet Lord, what were't to Thee
If there were no such worms as we?
Heaven ne'er the less still Heaven would be,
Should mankind dwell
In the deep hell.
What have his woes to do with Thee?
Let him go weep
O'er his own wounds;
Seraphims will not sleep,
Nor spheres let fall their faithful rounds.

Still would the youthful spirits sing;
And still Thy spacious palace ring;
Still would those beauteous ministers of light
Burn all as bright,
And bow their flaming heads before Thee;
Still Thrones and Dominations would adore Thee;
Still would those ever wakeful sons of fire
Keep warm Thy praise;
Both nights and days,
And teach Thy loved Name to their noble lyre.

Let froward Dust, then, do its kind,
And give itself for sport to the proud wind.
Why should a piece of peevish clay plead shares
In the Eternity of Thy old cares?
Why shouldst Thou bow Thy awful breast to see
What mine own madnesses have done with me?
Should not the king still keep his throne
Because some desperate fool's undone?
Or will the world's illustrious eyes
Weep for every worm that dies?

Will the gallant sun
E'er the less glorious run?
Will he hang down his golden head,
Or e'er the sooner seek his western bed,
Because some foolish fly
Grows wanton and will die?

If I were lost in misery,
What was it to Thy Heaven and Thee?
What was it to Thy precious Blood
If my foul heart called for a flood?
What if my faithless soul and I
Would needs fall in
With guilt and sin,
What did the Lamb that He should die
What did the Lamb that He should need,
When the wolf sins, Himself to bleed?
If my base lust
Bargained with death
And well beseeming dust,
Why should the white
Lamb's bosom write
The purple name
Of my sin's shame?

Why should His unstained Breast make good
My blushes with His own Heart Blood?
O, my Saviour, make me see
How dearly Thou hast paid for me,
That lost again my life may prove,
As then in death, so now in love.

On the Assumption of Our Lady

Hark! She is called; the parting hour is come;
Take thy farewell poor world, Heaven must go home.
A field of heavenly light, purer and brighter
Than the chaste stars whose choice lamps come to light her,
While through the crystal orbs, clearer than they,
She climbs, and makes a far more milky way.

She's called again; hark! how the immortal Dove
Sighs to His silver mate, 'Rise up My love;
Rise up My fair, My spotless one,
The winter's past, the rain is gone
The spring is come, the flowers appear,
No sweets but thou are wanting here.

Come away, My love;
Come away, My dove;
Cast off delay:
The court of Heaven is come,
To wait upon thee home;
Come away, come away,
The flowers appear,
Or quickly would, wert thou once here
The spring is come, or if it stay,
'Tis to keep time with thy delay.

The rain is gone, except so much
Detain in needful tears to weep the want of thee.
The winter's past;
Or, if he make less haste,
His answer is, 'Why she does so;
If summer come not how can winter go?
Come away, come away.'

She's called again, and will she go?
When Heaven bids come, who can say No?
Heaven calls her, and she must away:
Heaven will not, and she cannot stay.

Go then, go, glorious, on the golden wings
Of the bright youth of Heaven, that sings
Under so sweet a burden: go,
Since thy great Son will have it so:
And while thou goest, our song and we
Will, as we may reach after thee.

Hail holy queen of humble hearts.
We in thy praise will have our parts;
And though thy dearest looks must now be light
To none but the blest Heavens, whose bright
Beholders, lost in sweet delight,
Feed for ever their fair sight;
With those divinest eyes, which we
And our dark world shall no more see;

Though our poor joys are parted so,
Yet shall our lips never let go
Thy gracious name, but to the last
Our loving song shall hold it fast.
Thy sacred name shall be
Thyself to us, and we
With holy cares will keep it by us.
We to the last
Will hold it fast,
And no Assumption shall deny us.

All the sweetest showers
Of fairest flowers
We'll strew upon it:
Though our sweetness cannot make
It sweeter, they may take
Themselves new sweetness from it.

Maria, men and angels sing,
Maria, mother of our King.
Live rarest princess, and may the bright
Crown of a most incomparable light
Enhance thy radiant brows! O may the best
Of everlasting joys bathe thy white breast!
Live, our chaste love, the holy mirth
Of Heaven, the humble pride of earth:
Live, crown of women, queen of men;
Live, mistress of our song; and when
Our weak desires have done their best
Sweet angels come and sing the rest.

Vexilla Regis – (The Hymn of the Holy Cross)

i

Look up, languishing soul! Lo, where the fair
Badge of thy Faith calls back thy care,
And bids thee ne'er forget

Thy life is one long debt
Of love to Him, Who on this painful Tree
Paid back the flesh He took for thee.

ii

Lo, how the streams of life, from that full nest,
Of loves, Thy Lord's too liberal breast,
Flow in an amorous flood
Of water wedding blood.
With these He washed thy stain, transferred thy smart,
And took it home to His own Heart.

iii

But though great Love, greedy of such sad gain,
Usurped the portion of thy pain,
And from the nails and spear
Turned the steel point of fear:
Their use is changed, not. lost; and now they move
Not stings of wrath, but wounds of love.

iv

Tall Tree of life! thy truth makes good
What was till now ne'er understood,
Though the prophetic king
Struck loud his faithful string:
It was thy wood he meant should make the throne
For a more than Solomon.

v

Large throne of love, royally spread
With purple of too rich, a red,
Thy crime is too much duty,
Thy burden too much beauty.
Glorious or grievous more? Thus to make good
Thy costly excellence with thy King's own blood.

vi

Even balance of both worlds; our world of sin,
And that of grace, Heaven weighed in Him:
Us with our price thou weighest;
Our price for us thou payest,
Soon as the right-hand scale rejoiced to prove
How much Death weighed more light than Love.

vi

Hail, our alone hope! let thy fair head shoot
Aloft, and fill the nations with thy noble fruit:
The while our hearts and we
Thus graft ourselves on thee,
Grow thou and they. And be thy fair increase
The sinner's pardon and the just man's peace.

vii

Live, O for ever live and reign
The Lamb Whom His own love hath slain;
And let Thy lost sheep live to inherit
That kingdom which this Holy Cross did merit.
Amen.

*No man was able to answer him. Neither durst any man from
that day ask him any more question* – Matthew 22:46.

'Midst all the dark and knotty snares,
Black wit or malice can or dares,
Thy glorious wisdom breaks the nets,
And treads with uncontrolled steps.
Thy quelled foes are not only now
Thy triumphs, but Thy trophies too.
They both at once Thy conquests be,
And Thy conquests' memory.
Stony amazement makes them stand
Waiting on Thy victorious hand,
Like statues fixed to the fame
Of Thy renown, and their own shame,

As if they only meant to breathe,
To be the life of their own death.
'Twas time to hold their peace when they
Had ne'er another word to say:
Yet is their silence, unto Thee
The full sound of Thy victory;
Their silence speaks aloud, and is
Thy well pronounced panegyris.[1]
While they speak nothing, they speak all
Their share in Thy memorial.

1. Praise.

Divine epigrams

'Two Went Up into the Temple to Pray'

Two went to pray! O, rather say
One went to brag, the other to pray;
One stands up close and treads on high,
Where the other dares not send his eye.
One nearer to God's altar trod,
The other to the altar's God.

The Widow's Mites – Luke 21:2,3

Two mites, two drops (yet all her house and land)
Fall from a steady heart, though trembling hand:
The other's wanton wealth foams high and brave.
The other cast away; she only gave.

'I am Ready Not Only to be Bound But to Die' – Acts 21.13

Come death, come bonds, nor do you shrink, my ears,
At those hard words man's cowardice calls fears.
Save those of fear, no other bands fear I;
Nor other death than this – the fear to die.

Life for Death

So I may gain Thy death my life I'll give,
My life's Thy death and in Thy death I live;
Or else my life, I'll hide thee in His grave
By three days' loss eternally to save.

'Why are Ye Afraid, O Ye of Little Faith?' – Mark 4:40

As if the storm meant Him
Or 'cause Heaven's face is dim,
His needs a cloud.
Was ever forward wind
That could be so unkind,
Or wave so proud?
The wind had need be angry,
and the water black,
That to the mighty Neptune's self
Dare threaten wrack.

There is no storm but this
Of your own cowardice
That braves you out;
You are the storm that mocks
Yourselves; you are the rocks
Of your own doubt:
Besides this fear of danger,
There's no danger here
And he that here fears danger,
Does deserve his fear.

'Give to Caesar – and to God.' – Mark 12:17

All we have is God's, and yet
Caesar challenges a debt;
Nor hath God a thinner share
Whatever Caesar's payments are.
All is God's; and yet 'tis true
All we have is Caesar's too.

All is Caesar's: and what odds,
So long as Caesar's self is God's?

Upon the Holy Sepulchre.

Here, where our Lord once laid His head,
Now the grave lies buried.

Hymn to St Teresa [1]

Love, thou art absolute, sole Lord
Of life and death. To prove the word,
We'll now appeal to none of all
Those thy old soldiers, great and tall,
Ripe men of martyrdom, that could reach down
With strong arms their triumphant crown:
Such as could with lusty breath
Speak loud, unto the face of death,
Their great Lord's glorious name; to none
Of those whose spacious bosoms spread a throne
For love at large to fill. Spare blood and sweat:
We'll see Him take a private seat,
And make His mansion in the mild
And milky sod of a soft child.

Scarce has she learnt to lisp a name
Of martyr, yet she thinks it shame
Life should so long play with that breath
Which spent can buy so brave a death.
She never undertook to know
What death with love should have to do.
Nor has she e'er yet understood
Why, to show love, she should shed blood;
Yet, though she cannot tell you why,
She can love, and she can die.
Scarce has she blood enough to make
A guilty sword blush for her sake;
Yet has a heart dares hope to prove
How much less strong is death than love.

Since 'tis not to be had at home,
She'll travel for a martyrdom.
No home for her, confesses she,
But where she may a martyr be.
She'll to the Moors, and trade with them
For this unvalued diadem;
She offers them her dearest breath,
With Christ's name in it, in change for death:
She'll bargain with them, and will give
Them God, and teach them how to live
In Him; or, if they this deny,
For Him she'll teach them how to die.
So shall she leave amongst them sown
Her Lord's blood, or at least her own.

Farewell then, all the world, adieu!
Teresa is no more for you.
Farewell all pleasures, sports, and joys,
Never till now esteemed toys!
Farewell whatever dear may be –
Mother's arms, or father's knee!
Farewell house, and farewell home!
She's for the Moors and Martyrdom.

Sweet, not so fast; lo! Thy fair spouse,
Whom thou seek'st with so swift vows,
Calls thee back, and bids thee come
To embrace a milder martyrdom.

....

Those rare works, where thou shalt leave writ
Love's noble history, with wit
Taught thee by none but Him, while here
They feed our souls, shall clothe thine there.
Each heavenly word by whose hid flame
Our hard hearts shall strike fire, the same
Shall flourish on thy brows, and be

Both fire to us and flame to thee;
Whose light shall live bright in thy face
By glory, in our hearts by grace.
Thou shalt look round about, and see
Thousands of crowned souls throng to be
Themselves thy crown, sons of thy vows,
The virgin-births with which thy spouse
Made fruitful thy fair soul; go now,
And with them all about thee bow
To Him; put on, He'll say, put on,
My rosy Love, that thy rich zone,
Sparkling with the sacred flames
Of thousand souls, whose happy names
Heaven keeps upon thy score: thy bright
Life brought them first to kiss the light
That kindled them to stars; and so
Thou with the Lamb, thy Lord, shalt go.
And, wheresoe'er He sets His white
Steps, walk with Him those ways of light,
Which who in death would live to see,
Must learn in life to die like thee.

1. St Teresa of Avila, one of the great Spanish mystics of the Counter-
Reformation, and founder of the order of Discalced Carmelites. As a girl she
aimed to seek martyrdom deliberately by preaching to the Muslim Moors of
North Africa.

Upon the Book and Picture of the Seraphical St Teresa

O thou undaunted daughter of desires!
By all thy dower of lights and fires;
By all the eagle in thee, all the dove;
By all thy lives and deaths of love;
By thy large draughts of intellectual day,
And by thy thirsts of love more large than they;
By all thy brim-filled bowls of fierce desire,
By thy last morning's draught of liquid fire;
By the full kingdom of that final kiss
That seized thy parting soul, and sealed thee His;

By all the Heaven thou hast in Him
(Fair sister of the seraphim!);
By all of Him we have in thee
Leave nothing of myself in me.
Let me so read thy life, that I
Unto all life of mine may die!

A Letter to the Countess of Denbigh against Irresolution and Delay in Matters of Religion [1]

What heaven besieged heart is this
Stands trembling at the gate of bliss:
Holds fast the door, yet dares not venture
Fairly to open and to enter?
Whose definition is, A doubt
'Twixt life and death, 'twixt in and out.
Ah! linger not, loved soul: A slow
And late consent was a long no.
Who grants at last, a great while tried,
And did his best to have denied.
What magic-bolts, what mystic bars
Maintain the will in these strange wars?
What fatal, yet fantastic, bands
Keep the free heart from His own hands?
Say, lingering fair, why comes the birth
Of your brave soul so slowly forth?
Plead your pretences, (O you strong
In weakness) why you choose so long
In labour of your self to lie,
Not daring quite to live nor die.
So when the year takes cold we see
Poor waters their own prisoners be:
Fettered and locked up fast they lie
In a cold self-captivity.
The astonished nymphs their flood's strange fate deplore,
To find themselves their own severer shore.
Love, that lends haste to heaviest things
In you alone hath lost his wings.

Look round and read the world's wide face,
The field of nature or of grace;
Where can you fix, to find excuse
Or pattern for the pace you use?
Mark with what faith fruits answer flowers,
And know the call of heaven's kind showers:
Each mindful plant hastes to make good
The hope and promise of his bud.
Seed-time's not all; there should be harvest too.
Alas! And has the year no spring for you?

1. Susan, Countess of Denbigh was a sister of the Duke of Buckingham. She was
a Lady of the Bedchamber to Charles I's Queen Henrietta Maria. Eventually,
she became a Roman Catholic while in exile with the Royalist court.

Sir Edward Sherburne 1618-1692

Love

Love I'd of Heaven have bought when He, (this who
Would think?) both purchase was and seller too.
I offered gold, but gold He did not prize;
I offered gems, but gems He did despise;
I offered all; all He refused yet: 'Why,
If all won't take, take what is left,' said I.
At this He smiled, and said 'In vain divine
Love's price thou beatest; give nothing and she's thine.'

The Message

Dear Saviour, that my love I might make known
To Thee I sent more messengers than one.
My heart went first, but came not back; my will
I sent Thee next, and that stayed with Thee still;
Then, that the better Thou mightst know my mind,
I sent my intellect, that too stays behind.
Now my soul's sent: Lord, if that stay with Thee,
O what a happy carcase I shall be.

'Christus Matthaeum et Discipulos Alloquitur'
(Christ Addresses Matthew and the Disciples)

Leave, leave, converted publican! Lay down
That sinful trash, which in thy happier race,
To gain a heavenly crown,
Clogs thy free pace.
O! What for this pale dirt will not man do?
Nay, even now, amongst you
(For this) there's one I see,
Seeks to sell me.
But times will come hereafter, when for gold
I shall by more (alas!) than one be sold.

Conscience

Internal Cerberus, whose gripping fangs,
That gnaw the soul are the mind's secret pangs,
Thou greedy vulture that dost gorging tire
On hearts corrupted by impure desire.
Subtle and buzzing hornet! That dost ring
A peal of horror ere thou givest the sting.
The soul's rough file that smoothness does impart,
The hammer that does break a stony heart,
The worm that never dies! The thorn within
That pricks and pains: the whip and scourge of sin;
The voice of God in Man! Which without rest
Doth softly cry within a troubled breast
To all temptations is that soul left free
That makes not to itself a curb of me.

John Dryden 1631-1700

On Conversion (from The Hind and the Panther)

Be vengeance wholly left to powers divine,
And let Heaven judge betwixt your sons and mine:
If joys hereafter must be purchased here

With loss of all that mortals hold so dear,
Then welcome infamy and public shame,
And, last, a long farewell to worldly fame.
'Tis said with ease, but oh, how hardly tried
By haughty souls to human honour tied!
O sharp convulsive pangs of agonising pride!
Down them, thou rebel, never more to rise;
And what thou didst and dost so dearly prize,
That fame, that darling fame, make that thy sacrifice.
'Tis nothing thou hast given; then add thy tears
For a long race of unrepenting years:
'Tis nothing yet; yet all thou hast to give:
Then add those may-be years thou hast to live.
Yet nothing still: then poor and naked come,
Thy Father will receive his unthrift home,
And thy blest Saviour's blood discharge the mighty sum.

The Catholic Church (from *The Hind and the Panther*)

One in herself; not rent by schism, but sound,
Entire, one solid shining diamond,
Not sparkles shattered into sects like you:
One is the Church, and must be to be true,
One central principle of unity;
As undivided, so from errors free;
As one in faith, so one in sanctity.
Thus she, and none but she, the insulting rage
Of heretics opposed from age to age;
Still when the giant-brood invades her throne,
She stoops from heaven and meets them half way down,
And with paternal thunder vindicates her crown.
But like Egyptian sorcerers you stand,
And vainly lift aloft your magic wand
To sweep away the swarms of vermin from the land.
You could like them, with like infernal force,
Produce the plague, but not arrest the course.
But when the boils and botches with disgrace
And public scandal sat upon the face,

Themselves attacked, the Magi strove no more,
They saw God's finger, and their fate deplore;
Themselves they could not cure of the dishonest sore.
Thus one, thus pure, behold her largely spread,
Like the fair ocean from her mother-bed;
From east to west triumphantly she rides,
All shores are watered by her wealthy tides.
The gospel-sound, diffused from pole to pole,
Where winds can carry and where waves can roll,
The self-same doctrine of the sacred page
Conveyed to every clime, in every age.

Contradictory Witness (from *The Hind and the Panther*)

What weight of ancient witness can prevail
If private reason hold the public scale?
But, gracious God, how well dost Thou provide
For erring judgements an unerring guide?
Thy throne is darkness in the abyss of light,
A blaze of glory that forbids the sight;
O teach me to believe Thee thus concealed,
And search no farther than Thyself revealed;
But her alone for my director take
Whom Thou hast promised never to forsake!
My thoughtless youth was winged with vain desires,
My manhood, long misled by wandering fires,
Followed false lights; and when their glimpse was gone,
My pride struck out new sparkles of her own.
Such was I, such by nature still I am,
Be Thine the glory, and be mine the shame.
Good life be now my task: my doubts are done,
(What more could fright my faith, than Three in One?)
Can I believe eternal God could lie
Disguised in mortal mould and infancy?
That the great maker of the world could die?
And after that, trust my imperfect sense
Which calls in question his omnipotence?
Can I my reason to my faith compel,

And shall my sight, and touch, and taste rebel?
Superior faculties are set aside,
Shall their subservient organs be my guide?
Then let the moon usurp the rule of day,
And winking tapers show the sun his way;
For what my senses can themselves perceive
I need no revelation to believe.
Can they who say the Host should be descried
By sense, define a body glorified?
Impassible, and penetrating parts?
Let them declare by what mysterious arts
He shot that body through the opposing might
Of bolts and bars impervious to the light,
And stood before his train confessed in open sight.
For since thus wondrously he passed, 'tis plain
One single place two bodies did contain,
And sure the same omnipotence as well
Can make one body in more places dwell.
Let reason then at her own quarry fly,
But how can finite grasp infinity?
'Tis urged again that faith did first commence
By miracles, which are appeals to sense,
And thence concluded that our sense must be
The motive still of credibility.
For latter ages must on former wait,
And what began belief, must propagate.
But winnow well this thought, and you shall find,
'Tis light as chaff that flies before the wind.
Were all those wonders wrought by power divine
As means or ends of some more deep design?
Most sure as means, whose end was this alone,
To prove the God-head of the eternal Son.
God thus asserted: man is to believe
Beyond what sense and reason can conceive.
And for mysterious things of faith rely
On the proponent, Heaven's authority.
If then our faith we for our guide admit,

Vain is the farther search of human wit,
As when the building gains a surer stay,
We take the unuseful scaffolding away:
Reason by sense no more can understand,
The game is played into another hand.
Why choose we then like *Bilanders* to creep [1]
Along the coast, and land in view to keep,
When safely we may launch into the deep?
In the same vessel which our Saviour bore
Himself the pilot, let us leave the shore,
And with a better guide a better world explore.
Could He his god-head veil with flesh and blood
And not veil these again to be our food?
His grace in both is equal in extent,
The first affords us life, the second nourishment.
And if he can, why all this frantic pain
To construe what his clearest words contain,
And make a riddle what he made so plain?
To take up half on trust, and half to try,
Name it not faith, but bungling bigotry.
Both knave and fool the merchant we may call
To pay great sums, and to compound the small.
For who would break with heaven, and would not break
   for all?
Rest then, my soul, from endless anguish freed;
Nor sciences thy guide, nor sense thy creed.
Faith is the best insurer of thy bliss;
The Bank above must fail before the venture miss.
But heaven and heaven-born faith are far from Thee
Thou first Apostate to Divinity.

1. Bilanders = small vessels.

Veni Creator Spiritus

Creator Spirit, by whose aid
The world's foundations first were laid,
Come visit every pious mind;
Come pour Thy joys on humankind;

From sin and sorrow set us free,
And make Thy temples worthy thee.
O source of uncreated light,
The Father's promised Paraclete!
Thrice holy font, thrice holy fire,
Our hearts with heavenly love inspire;
Come, and Thy sacred unction bring
To sanctify us while we sing!
Plenteous of grace, descend from high,
Rich in Thy sevenfold energy,
Thou strength of His almighty hand,
Whose power does heaven and earth command!
Proceeding Spirit, our defence,
Who dost the gift of tongues dispense,
And crownst Thy gift with eloquence!
Refine and purge our earthy parts;
But, O, inflame and fire our hearts!
Our frailties help, our vice control,
Submit the senses to the soul;
And when rebellious they are grown,
Then lay thy hand and hold them down.
Chase from our minds the infernal foe,
And peace, the fruit of love, bestow;
And lest our feet should step astray,
Protect and guide us in the way.
Make us eternal truths receive,
And practise all that we believe:
Give us thyself that we may see
The Father and the Son, by Thee.
Immortal honour, endless fame,
Attend the Almighty Father's Name:
The Saviour Son be glorified,
Who for lost man's redemption died;
And equal adoration be,
Eternal Paraclete, to Thee.

The Weight of Tradition (from *Religio Laici*)

Oh but says one, tradition set aside,
Where can we hope for an unerring guide?
For since the original scripture has been lost,
All copies disagreeing, maimed the most,
Or Christian faith can have no certain ground,
Or truth in Church tradition must be found.
Such an omniscient Church we wish indeed;
'Twere worth both Testaments, and cast in the Creed
But if this mother be a guide so sure,
As can all doubts resolve, all truth secure,
Then her infallibility, as well
Where copies are corrupt, or lame, can tell;
Restore lost canon with as little pains,
As truly explicate what still remains:
Which yet no council dare pretend to do;
Unless like Esdras, they could write it new:
Strange confidence, still to interpret true,
Yet not be sure that all they have explained,
Is in the blessed original contained.
More safe, and much more modest 'tis, to say
God would not leave Mankind without a way:
And that the Scriptures, though not every where
Free from corruption, or entire, or clear,
Are incorrupt, sufficient, clear, entire,
In all things which our needful Faith require.
If others in the same glass better see
'Tis for themselves they look, but not for me:
For my salvation must its doom receive
Not from what others, but what I believe.
Must all tradition then be set aside?
This to affirm were ignorance, or pride.
Are there not many points, some needful sure
To saving faith, that Scripture leaves obscure?
Which every sect will wrest a several way
(For what one sect interprets, all sects may:)
We hold, and say we prove from Scripture plain,

That Christ is GOD; the bold Socinian [1]
From the same Scripture urges He's but Man.
Now what appeal can end the important suit;
Both parts talk loudly, but the rule is mute?
Shall I speak plain, and in a nation free
Assume an honest layman's liberty?
I think according to my little skill,
To my own Mother-Church submitting still:)
That many have been saved, and many may,
Who never heard this question brought in play.
The unlettered Christian, who believes in gross,
Plods on to Heaven; and never is at a loss:
For the straight-gate would be made straighter yet,
Were none admitted there but men of wit.
The few, by nature formed, with learning fraught,
Born to instruct, as others to be taught,
Must study well the sacred page; and see
Which doctrine, this, or that, does best agree
With the whole tenor of the work divine:
And plainest points to heaven's revealed design:
Which exposition flows from genuine sense;
And which is forced by wit and eloquence.
Not that tradition's parts are useless here:
When general, old, disinterested and clear:
That ancient fathers thus expound the page,
Gives truth the reverend majesty of age:
Confirms its force, by biding every test;
For best authority's next rules are best.
And still the nearer to the spring we go
More limpid, more unsoiled the waters flow.
Thus, first traditions were a proof alone;
Could we be certain such they were, so known:
But since some flaws in long descent may be,
They make not truth but probability.
Even Arius and Pelagius durst provoke
To what the centuries preceding spoke.
Such difference is there in an oft-told tale:

But truth by its own sinews will prevail.
Tradition written therefore more commends
Authority, than what from voice descends:
And this, as perfect as its kind can be,
Rolls down to us the sacred history:
Which, from the universal church received,
Is tried, and after, for its self believed.

1. Faustus Socinius, 1539-1604, precursor of Unitarians in denying the divinity of Christ.

Anne Killigrew 1660-1685

On Death

Tell me thou safest end of all our woe,
Why wretched mortals do avoid thee so:
Thou gentle drier of the afflicted's tears,
Thou noble ender of the coward's fears;
Thou sweet repose to lovers' sad despair,
Thou calm to ambition's rough tempestuous care.
If in regard of bliss thou wert a curse,
And than the joys of Paradise art worse;
Yet after man from his first station fell,
And God from Eden Adam did expel,
Thou wert no more an evil, but relief;
The balm and cure to every human grief:
Through thee, what man had forfeited before
He now enjoys, and ne'er can lose it more.
No subtle serpents in the grave betray,
Worms on the body there, not souls, do prey;
No vice there tempts, no terrors there affright,
No cozening sin affords a false delight:
No vain contentions do that peace annoy,
No fierce alarms break the lasting day.
Ah since from thee so many blessings flow,
Such real good as life can never know;
Come when thou wilt, in thy affrighting'st dress,
Thy shape shall never make thy welcome less.

Thou may'st to joy, but ne'er to fear give birth,
Thou best, as well as certain'st thing on earth.
Fly thee? May travellers then fly their rest,
And hungry infants fly the proffered breast.
No, those that faint and tremble at thy name,
Fly from their good on a mistaken fame.
Thus childish fear did Israel of old
From plenty and the Promised Land with-hold;
They fancied giants, and refused to go
When Canaan did with milk and honey flow.

Alexander Pope (1688-1744)

The Temptation of Riches

Where London's column, pointing at the skies,
Like a tall bully, lifts the head and lies, [1]
There dwelt a citizen of sober fame,
A plain good man, and Balaam was his name;
Religious, punctual, frugal, and so forth;
His word would pass for more than he was worth.
One solid dish his week-day meal affords,
An added pudding solemnized the Lord's:
Constant at Church and Change; his gains were sure, [2]
His givings rare, save farthings to the poor.
The Devil was piqued such saintship to behold,
And longed to tempt him like good Job of old:
But Satan now is wiser than of yore,
And tempts by making rich, not making poor.
Roused by the Prince of Air, the whirlwinds sweep
The surge and plunge his father in the deep;
Then full against his Cornish lands they roar,
And two rich ship-wrecks bless the lucky shore.
Sir Balaam now, he lives like other folks,
He takes his chirping pint, and cracks his jokes:
'Live like yourself', was soon my Lady's word;
And lo! two puddings smoked upon the board.

Asleep and naked as an Indian lay,
An honest factor stole a gem away:
He pledged it to the knight; the knight had wit,
So kept the diamond, but the rogue was bit.
Some scruple rose, but thus he eased his thought,
'I'll now give sixpence where I gave a groat,
Where once I went to church, I'll now go twice –
And am so clear too of all other vice.'
The Tempter saw his time; the work he plied;
Stocks and subscriptions pour on every side,
Till all the Demon makes his full descent
In one abundant shower of cent per cent,
Sinks deep within him, and possesses whole,
Then dubs Director, and secures his soul.
Behold Sir Balaam, now a man of spirit,
Ascribes his gettings to his parts and merit,
What late he called a blessing, now was wit,
And God's good Providence, a lucky hit.
Things change their titles, as our manners turn:
His counting house employed the Sunday morn
Seldom at church ('twas such a busy life)
But duly sent his family and wife.
There (so the Devil ordained) one Christmas-tide
My good old Lady catched a cold, and died.
A nymph of quality admires our Knight;
He marries, bows at Court, and grows polite:
Leaves the dull City, and joins (to please the fair)
The well-bred cuckolds in St James' air:
First, for his son, a gay commission buys,
Who drinks, whores, fights, and in a duel dies:
His daughter flaunts, a Viscount's tawdry wife;
She bears a coronet and pox for life.[3]
In Britain's senate he a seat obtains,
And one more pensioner St Stephen gains.
My Lady falls to play; so bad her chance,
He must repair it; takes a bribe from France;
The House impeach him; Coningsby harangues;

The Court forsake him, and Sir Balaam hangs:
Wife, son, and daughter, Satan, are thy own,
His wealth, yet dearer, forfeit to the Crown:
The Devil and the King divide the prize,
And sad Sir Balaam curses God and dies.

1. The newly-built Monument ascribed the Great Fire of London to Papists.
2. Change = Stock Exchange. 3. Pox = syphilis.

Fate (from *The Essay on Man*)

Heaven from all creatures hides the book of fate,
All but the page prescribed, their present state
From brutes what men, from men what spirits know:
Or who could suffer being here below?
The lamb thy riot dooms to bleed to-day,
Had he thy reason, would he skip and play?
Pleased to the last, he crops the flowery food,
And licks the hand just raised to shed his blood.
Oh blindness to the future! Kindly given,
That each may fill the circle marked by Heaven:
Who sees with equal eye, as God of all,
A hero perish, or a sparrow fall.
Atoms or systems into ruin hurled,
And now a bubble burst, and now a world.
Hope humbly then; with trembling pinions soar;
Wait the great teacher death, and God adore.
What future bliss, he gives not thee to know,
But gives that hope to be thy blessing now.
Hope springs eternal in the human breast:
Man never is, but always to be blest.
The soul (uneasy, and confined) from home,
Rests and expatiates in a life to come.

Let earth unbalanced from her orbit fly,
Planets and stars run lawless through the sky;
Let ruling angels from their spheres be hurled,

Being on being wrecked, and world on world;
Heaven's whole foundations to their centre nod,
And nature trembles to the throne of God.
All this dread order break – for whom? For thee?
Vile worm! Oh madness! Pride! Impiety!
What if the foot, ordained the dust to tread,
Or hand, to toil, aspired to be the head?
What if the head, the eye, or ear repined
To serve mere engines to the ruling mind?
Just as absurd for any part to claim
To be another, in this general frame:
Just as absurd, to mourn the tasks or pains,
The great directing mind of all ordains.
All are but parts of one stupendous whole,
Whose body nature is, and God the soul;
That, changed through all, and yet in all the same;
Great in the earth, as in the ethereal frame
Warms in the sun, refreshes in the breeze,
Glows in the stars, and blossoms in the trees,
Lives through all life, extends through all extent,
Spreads undivided, operates unspent;
Breathes in our soul, informs our mortal part,
As full, as perfect, in a hair as heart;
As full, as perfect, in vile man that mourns,
As the rapt seraph, that adores and burns:
To him no high, no low, no great, no small;
He fills, he bounds, connects, and equals all.
Cease then, nor order imperfection name:
Our proper bliss depends on what we blame.
Know thy own point: This kind, this due degree
Of blindness, weakness, heaven bestows on thee.
Submit. In this, or any other sphere,
Secure to be as blest as thou canst bear:
Safe in the hand of one disposing power,
Or in the natal, or the mortal hour.
All nature is but art, unknown to thee;
All chance, direction, which thou canst not see;

All discord, harmony not understood;
All partial evil, universal good:
And, spite of pride, in erring reason's spite,
One truth is clear. Whatever is, is right.

Know Then Thyself (from The Essay on Man)

Know then thyself, presume not God to scan;
The proper study of mankind is man.
Placed on this isthmus of a middle state,
A being darkly wise, and rudely great;
With too much knowledge for the sceptic side –
With too much weakness for the stoic's pride,
He hangs between; in doubt to act, or rest;
In doubt to deem himself a God, or beast;
In doubt his mind or body to prefer;
Born but to die, and reasoning but to err;
Alike in ignorance, his reason such,
Whether he thinks too little, or too much;
Chaos of thought and passion, all confused;
Still by himself abused, or disabused;
Created half to rise, and half to fall;
Great lord of all things, yet a prey to all;
Sole judge of truth, in endless error hurled:
The glory, jest, and riddle of the world!

The Nun (from Eloise and Abelard)

How happy is the blameless vestal's lot!
The world forgetting, by the world forgot:
Eternal sunshine of the spotless mind!
Each prayer accepted, and each wish resigned,
Labour and rest that equal periods keep:
'Obedient slumbers that can wake and weep':
Desires composed, affections ever even;
Tears that delight, and sighs that waft to Heaven
Grace shine around her with serenest beams,
And whispering angels prompt her golden dreams;

For her the unfading rose of Eden blooms,
And wings of seraphs shed divine perfumes;
For her the spouse prepares the bridal ring,
For her white virgins hymeneals sing;
To sounds of heavenly harps she dies away,
And melts in visions of eternal day.

The Dying Christian to His Soul

Vital Spark of heavenly flame
Quit, O quit this mortal frame:
Trembling, hoping, lingering, flying,
O the pain, the bliss of dying.
Cease, fond Nature cease thy strife,
And let me languish into life.

Hark! They whisper. Angels say:-
'Sister Spirit, come away!'
What is this absorbs me quite?
Steals my senses, shuts my sight,
Drowns my spirit, draws my breath?
Tell me, my soul, can this be death?

The world recedes; it disappears!
Heaven opens on my eyes! My ears
With sounds seraphic ring!
Lend, lend your wings! I mount! I fly!
O Grave, where is thy victory?
O Death, where is thy sting?

Hymn

Thou art my God, sole object of my love;
Not for the hope of endless joys above
Not for the fear of endless pains below,
Which they who love Thee not must undergo.
For me, and such as me, Thou deignst to bear
An ignominious Cross, the nails, the spear:

A thorny crown transpierced Thy sacred brow
While bloody sweats from every member flow.
For me in tortures Thou resign'st Thy breath,
Embraced me on the Cross, and saved me by Thy death.
And can these sufferings fail my heart to move?
What but thyself can now deserve my love?
Such as then was, and is, Thy love to me,
Such is, and shall be still, my love to Thee –
To thee, Redeemer! Mercy's sacred spring!
My God, my Father, Maker, and my King!

PART IV

Second Spring
1850-1900

English Catholicism was at a low ebb from the end of the seventeenth century, and this is reflected in the dearth of Catholic poetry written after Pope's death in 1744. From 1685 to 1850 England was recognised as a missionary region, being administered by a Vicar General. However, many of the penal laws were repealed by the Catholic Emancipation Act of 1829, which was followed by the restoration of the Hierarchy in 1850. The same period also saw the 'Second Spring' of the revival of Catholic life, letters, and education led by converts such as Newman and Manning. Indeed, poets of the stature of Coventry Patmore, Alice Meynell, and Francis Thompson, as well as the (then unpublished) Gerard Manley Hopkins, made it probably the greatest period for Catholic verse in English.

John Henry, Cardinal Newman 1801-1890

Heavenly Leadings

Did we but see,
When life first opened, how our journey lay
Between its earliest and its closing day,
Or view ourselves, as we one time shall be,
Who strive for the high prize, such sight would break
The youthful spirit, though bold for Jesus' sake.

But Thou, dear Lord!
Whilst I traced out bright scenes which were to come,
Isaac's pure blessings, and a verdant home,
Didst spare me, and withhold Thy fearful word;
Willing me year by year till I am found
A pilgrim pale with Paul's sad girdle bound.

The Pillar of the Cloud (Lead, Kindly Light)

Lead, kindly light, amid the encircling gloom,
Lead Thou me on!
The night is dark, and I am far from home –
Lead Thou me on!
Keep Thou my feet; I do not ask to see
The distant scene – one step enough for me.

I was not ever thus, nor prayed that Thou
Shouldst lead me on.
I loved to choose and see my path; but now
Lead Thou me on!
I loved the garish day, and, spite of fears,
Pride ruled my will; remember not past years.

So long Thy power hath blessed me, sure it still
Will lead me on,
O'er moor and fen, o'er crag and torrent, till
The night is gone;
And with the morn those angel faces smile
Which I have loved long since, and lost awhile.

The Dream of Gerontius (extract)

Jesu, Maria, – I am near to death,
And Thou art calling me; I know it now –
Not by the token of this faltering breath,
This chill at heart, this dampness on my brow.
(Jesu, have mercy! Mary, pray for me!) –
'Tis this new feeling, never felt before,
(Be with me, Lord, in my extremity!)
That I am going, that I am no more.
'Tis this strange innermost abandonment,
(Lover of souls ! Great God! I look to Thee.)
This emptying out of each constituent
And natural force, by which I come to be.
Pray for me, O my friends; a visitant
Is knocking his dire summons at my door,
The like of whom, to scare me and to daunt,
Has never, never come to me before;
'Tis death – O loving friends, your prayers! –

'Tis he! ...
As though my very being had given way,
As though I was no more a substance now,
And could fall back on nought to be my stay,
(Help, loving Lord! Thou my sole Refuge, Thou)
And turn no whither, but must needs decay
And drop from out the universal frame
Into that shapeless, scopeless, blank abyss,
That utter nothingness, of which I came:
This is it that has come to pass in me;
O horror! This is it, my dearest, this;
So pray for me, my friends, who have not strength to pray.

The Sign of the Cross

Whenever across this sinful flesh of mine,
I draw the Holy Sign,
All good thoughts stir within me, and renew
Their slumbering strength divine;

Till there springs up a courage high and true
To suffer and to do.

And who shall say, but hateful spirits around,
For their brief hour unbound,
Shudder to see, and wail their overthrow?
While on far heathen ground
Some lonely saint hails the fresh odour, though
Its source he cannot know.

Relics of the Saints

'The Fathers are in dust, yet live to God'
So says the Truth; as if the motionless clay
Still held the seeds of life beneath the sod,
Smouldering and straggling till the judgement day.

And hence we learn with reverence to esteem
Of these frail houses, though the grave confines;
Sophist may urge his cunning tests, and deem
That they are earth – but they are heavenly shrines.

Firmly I Believe and Truly

Firmly I believe and truly
God is three, and God is one,
And I next acknowledge, duly
Manhood taken by the Son.

And I trust and hope most fully
In that manhood crucified;
And each thought and deed unruly
Do to death, as he has died.

Simply to his grace and wholly
Light and life and strength belong;
And I love supremely, solely,
Him the holy, Him the strong.

And I hold in veneration,
For the love of him alone,
Holy Church, as his creation,
And her teachings, as his own.

Adoration aye be given,
With and through the angelic host,
To the God of earth and heaven,
Father, Son and Holy Ghost.

Help, Lord, the Souls that Thou Hast Made!

Help, Lord, the souls that thou hast made,
The souls to thee so dear;
In prison for the debt unpaid
Of sin committed here.

These holy souls, they suffer on,
Resigned in heart and will,
Until thy high behest is done,
And justice has its fill.

For daily falls, for pardoned crime
They joy to undergo
The shadow of thy Cross sublime,
The remnant of thy woe.

Oh, by their patience of delay,
Their hope amid their pain,
Their sacred zeal to burn away
Disfigurement and stain.

Oh, by their fire of love,
Not less in keenness than the flame;
Oh, by their very helplessness,
Oh, by thy own great name.

Good Jesus, help! Sweet Jesus aid
The souls to thee most dear,
In prison for the debt unpaid
Of sins committed here.

R.S. Hawker 1803-1875

A Christ-Cross Rhyme

Christ His Cross shall be my speed!
Teach me, Father John, to read,
That in Church on Holy day
I may chant the psalm and pray.

Let me learn, that I may know
What the shining windows show:
Where the lovely Lady stands,
With that bright Child in her hands.

Teach me letters, A, B, C,
Till that I shall able be
Signs to know and words to frame,
And to spell sweet Jesus' Name.

Then, dear Master, will I look
Day and night in that fair book
Where the tales of saints are told,
With their pictures, all in gold.

Teach me, Father John, to say
Vesper-verse and Matin-lay;
So when I to God shall plead,
Christ His Cross shall be my speed.

'I am the Resurrection and the Life', saith the Lord!

We stood beside an opening grave,
By fair Morwenna's walls of grey:
Our hearts were hushed – the God who gave
Had called a sister-soul away.
Hark! What wild tones around us float:
The chanting cuckoo's double note!

We uttered there the solemn sound –
'Man that is born from flesh of Eve,
The banished flower of Eden's ground,
Hath but a little time to live'; –
And still, amid each pausing word,
The strange cry of that secret bird.

'Ashes to ashes – dust to dust'–
The last farewell we sadly said.
Our mighty hope – our certain trust –
The resurrection of the dead.
Again, all air, it glides around,
A voice! – The spirit of a sound.

A doctrine dwells in that deep tone;
A truth is borne on yonder wing;
Long years! Long years! The note is known –
The blessed messenger of spring!
Thus saith that pilgrim of the skies:
'Lo! All that dieth shall arise!'

Rejoice! Though dull with wintry gloom
Love's sepulchre and sorrow's night,
The sun shall visit depth and tomb
A season of eternal light!
Like the glad bosom of the rose,
The mound shall burst – the grave unclose!

Yea! Soothed by that unvarying song
What generations here have trod!
What winds have breathed that sound along,
Fit signal of the changeless God!
Hark! Yet again the echoes float,
The chanting cuckoo's double note!

Aunt Mary: A Christmas Chant

Now, of all the trees by the king's highway,
Which do you love the best?
O! The one that is green upon Christmas Day,
The bush with the bleeding breast.
Now the holly with her drops of blood for me:
For that is our dear Aunt Mary's tree.

Its leaves are sweet with our Saviour's Name,
'Tis a plant that loves the poor:
Summer and winter it shines the same
Beside the cottage door.
O! The holly with her drops of blood for me:
For that is our kind Aunt Mary's tree.

'Tis a bush that the birds will never leave:
They sing in it all day long;
But sweetest of all upon Christmas Eve
Is to hear the robin's song.
'Tis the merriest sound upon earth or sea:
For it comes from our own Aunt Mary's tree.

So, of all that grows by the king's highway,
I love that tree the best;
'Tis a bower for the birds upon Christmas Day,
The bush of the bleeding breast.
O! The holly with her drops of blood for me:
For that is our sweet Aunt Mary's tree.

Aishah Shechinah [1]

A shape, like folded light, embodied air,
Yet wreathed with flesh, and warm;
All that of Heaven is feminine and fair,
Moulded in visible form.

She stood, the Lady Shechinah of Earth,
A chancel for the sky;
Where woke, to breath and beauty, God's own birth,
For men to see Him by.

Round her, too pure to mingle with the day,
Light, that was Life, abode;
Folded within her fibres meekly lay
The link of boundless God.

So linked, so blent, that when, with pulse fulfilled,
Moved but that infant Hand,
Far, far away, His conscious Godhead thrilled,
And stars might understand.

Lo! Where they pause, with intergathering rest,
The Threefold and the One!
And lo! He binds them to her orient breast,
His Manhood girded on.

The Zone, where two glad worlds forever meet,
Beneath that bosom ran:
Deep in that womb, the conquering Paraclete
Smote Godhead on to man!

Sole scene among the stars, where, yearning, glide
The Threefold and the One:
Her God upon her lap, the Virgin-Bride,
Her awful Child: her Son.

1. Hebrew: Our Lady as 'the Pillar of the Cloud'.

James Clarence Mangan 1803-1849

St Patrick's Hymn before Tarah (from the Gaelic)

At Tarah to-day, in this awful hour,
I call on the Holy Trinity:

Glory to Him who reigneth in power,
The God of the elements, Father and Son
And Paraclete Spirit, which Three are the One,
The ever-existing Divinity!

At Tarah to-day I call on the Lord,
On Christ, the omnipotent Word,
Who came to redeem us from death and sin
Our fallen race:
And I put and I place
The virtue that lieth and liveth in
His incarnation lowly,
His baptism pure and holy,
His life of toil and tears and affliction,
His dolorous death – His crucifixion,
His burial, sacred and sad and lone,
His resurrection to life again,
His glorious ascension to Heaven's high throne,
And lastly, His future dread
And terrible coming to judge all men –
Both the living and dead.

At Tarah to-day I put and I place
The virtue that dwells in the seraphim's love,
And the virtue and grace
That are in the obedience
And unshaken allegiance
Of all the archangels and angels above,
And in the hope of the resurrection
To everlasting reward and election.
And in the prayers of the fathers of old,
And in the truths the prophets foretold,
And in the Apostles' manifold preachings,
And in the confessors' faith and teachings;
And in the purity ever dwelling
Within the immaculate Virgin's breast,
And in the actions bright and excelling
Of all good men, the just and the blest.

At Tarah to-day, in this fateful hour,
I place all heaven within its power,
And the sun with its brightness,
And the snow with its whiteness,
And fire with all the strength it hath,
And lightning with its rapid wrath,
And the winds with their swiftness along their path,
And the sea with its deepness,
And the rocks with their steepness,
And the earth with its darkness –
All these I place,
By God's almighty help and grace,
Between myself and the powers of darkness.

At Tarah to-day
May God be my stay!
May the strength of God now nerve me!
May the power of God preserve me!
May God the Almighty be near me!
May God the Almighty espy me!
May God the Almighty hear me!
May God give me eloquent speech!
May the arm of God protect me!
May the wisdom of God direct me!
May God give me power to teach and to preach!

May the shield of God defend me!
May the host of God attend me,
And ward me,
And guard me
Against the wiles of demons and devils,
Against the temptations of vices and evils,
Against the bad passions and wrathful will
Of the reckless mind and the wicked heart –
Against every man who designs me ill,
Whether leagued with others or plotting apart!

In this hour of hours, I place all those powers
Between myself and every foe
Who threaten my body and soul
With danger or dole,
To protect me against the evils that flow
From lying soothsayers' incantations,
From the gloomy laws of the Gentile nations,
From heresy's hateful innovations,
From idolatry's rites and invocations.
Be these my defenders,
My guards against every ban –
And spell of smiths, and Druids, and women;
In fine, against every knowledge that renders
The light Heaven sends us dim in
The spirit and soul of man!

May Christ, I pray,
Protect me to-day
Against poison and fire,
Against drowning and wounding;
That so, in His grace abounding,
I may earn the preacher's hire!

Christ as a light
Illumine and guide me!
Christ as a shield o'ershadow and cover me!
Christ be under me!
Christ be over me!
Christ be beside me,
On the left hand and right!
Christ be before me, behind me, about me;
Christ this day be within and without me!

Christ, the lowly and meek,
Christ the All-Powerful be
In the heart of each to whom I speak,
In the mouth of each who speaks to me!

In all who draw near me,
To see me or hear me!

At Tarah to-day, in this awful hour,
I call on the Holy Trinity!
Glory to Him who reigneth in power,
The God of the elements, Father and Son
And Paraclete Spirit, which Three are the One,
The ever-existing Divinity!

Salvation dwells with the Lord,
With Christ, the omnipotent Word.
From generation to generation
Grant us, O Lord, Thy grace and salvation!

Aubrey De Vere 1814-1902

Sorrow

Count each affliction, whether light or grave,
God's messenger sent down to thee; do thou
With courtesy receive him; rise and bow;
And, ere his shadow pass thy threshold, crave
Permission first His heavenly feet to lave;
Then lay before Him all thou hast; allow
No cloud or passion to usurp thy brow,
Or mar thy hospitality; no wave
Of mortal tumult to obliterate
Thy soul's marmoreal calmness. Grief should be
Like joy, majestic, equable, sedate;
Confirming, cleansing, raising, making free;
Strong to consume small troubles; to commend
Great thoughts, grave thoughts, thoughts lasting to the end.

Human Life

Sad is our youth, for it is ever going,
Crumbling away beneath our very feet;
Sad is our life, for onward it is flowing,

In current unperceived because so fleet;
Sad are our hopes, for they were sweet in sowing,
But tares, self-sown, have overtopped the wheat;
Sad are our joys, for they were sweet in blowing;
And still, O still, their dying breath is sweet;
And sweet is youth, although it hath bereft us
Of that which made our childhood sweeter still;
And sweeter our life's decline, for it hath left us
A nearer good to cure an older ill;
And sweet are all things, when we learn to prize them
Not for their sake, but His who grants them or denies them.

Implicit Faith

Of all great nature's tones that sweep
Earth's resonant bosom, far or near,
Low-breathed or loudest, shrill or deep,
How few are grasped by mortal ear.

Ten octaves close our scale of sound:
Its myriad grades, distinct or twined,
Transcend our hearing's petty bound,
To us as colours to the blind.

In Sound's unmeasured empire thus
The heights, the depths alike we miss;
Ah, but in measured sound to us
A compensating spell there is!

In holy music's golden speech
Remotest notes to notes respond:
Each octave is a world; yet each
Vibrates to worlds its own beyond.

Our narrow pale the vast resumes;
Our seashell whispers of the sea:
Echoes are ours of angel-plumes
That winnow far infinity!

Clasp thou of Truth the central core! –
Hold fast that centre's central sense!
An atom there shall fill thee more
Than realms on Truth's circumference.

It cradled Saviour, mute and small,
Was God – is God while worlds endure!
Who holds Truth truly holds it all
In essence, or in miniature.

Know what thou know'st! He knoweth much
Who knows not many things: and he
Knows most whose knowledge hath a touch
Of God's divine simplicity.

Fr Frederick Faber 1814-1863

Our Lady in the Middle Ages

I looked upon the earth: it was a floor
For noisy pageant and rude bravery –
Wassail, and arms, and chase, among the high,
And burning hearts uncheered among the poor;
And gentleness from every land withdrew.
Methought that beds of whitest lilies grew
All suddenly upon the earth, in bowers;
And gentleness, that wandered like a wind,
And nowhere could meet sanctuary find,
Passed like a dewy breath into the flowers.
Earth heeded not; she still was tributary
To kings and knights, and man's heart well-nigh failed;
Then were the natural charities exhaled
Afresh, from out the blessed love of Mary.

Faith of Our Fathers

Faith of our fathers, living still
In spite of dungeon, fire and sword;

Oh, how our hearts
Beat high with joy
Whene'er we hear that glorious word!

Faith of our fathers! Holy Faith!
We will be true to thee till death,
We will be true to thee till death.

Our fathers, chained in prisons dark,
Were still in heart
And conscience free;
How sweet would be their children's fate,
If they, like them, could die for thee!

Faith of our fathers, Mary's prayers,
Shall win our country back to thee;
And through the truth that comes from God
England shall then indeed be free.

Faith of our fathers, we will love both
Friend and foe in all our strife,
And preach thee too, as love knows how,
By kindly words and virtuous life.

Faith of our fathers! Holy Faith!
We will be true to thee till death,
We will be true to thee till death.

The Right Must Win

Oh, it is hard to work for God,
To rise and take His part
Upon this battlefield of earth,
And not sometimes lose heart.

He hides Himself so wondrously,
As though there were no God;

184

He is least seen when all the powers
Of ill are most abroad.

Or He deserts us at the hour
The fight is all but lost;
And seems to leave us to ourselves
Just when we need Him most.

Ill masters good; good seems to change
To ill with greatest ease;
And, worst of all, the good with good
Is at cross-purposes.

Ah! God is other than we think;
His ways are far above,
Far beyond reason's height, and reached
Only by child-like love.

Workman of God! Oh, lose not heart,
But learn what God is like;
And in the darkest battlefield
Thou shalt know where to strike.

Thrice blessed is he to whom is given
The instinct that can tell
That God is on the field when He
Is most invisible.

Blessed, too, is he who can divine
Where real right doth lie,
And dares to take the side that seems
Wrong to man's blindfold eye.

For right is right, since God is God;
And right the day must win;
To doubt would be disloyalty,
To falter would be sin.

Coventry Patmore 1823-1896

Victory in Defeat

Ah, God, alas,
How soon it came to pass
The sweetness melted from Thy barbed hook
Which I so simply took;
And I lay bleeding on the bitter land,
Afraid to stir against Thy least command,
But losing all my pleasant life-blood, whence
Force should have been heart's frailty to withstand.
Life is not life at all without delight,
Nor has it any might;
And better than the insentient heart and brain
Is sharpest pain;
And better for the moment seems it to rebel,
If the great Master, from His lifted seat,
Ne'er whispers to the wearied servant 'Well!'
Yet what returns of love did I endure,
When to be pardoned seemed almost more sweet
Than aye to have been pure!
But day still faded to disastrous night,
And thicker darkness changed to feebler light,
Until forgiveness, without stint renewed,
Was now no more with loving tears imbued,
Vowing no more offence.
Not less to Thine Unfaithful didst Thou cry,
'Come back, poor Child; be all as 'twas before.'
But I,
'No, no; I will not promise any more! –
Yet, when I feel my hour is come to die,
And so I am secured of continence,
Then may I say, though haply then in vain,
'My only, only Love, O, take me back again!'
Thereafter didst Thou smite
So hard that, for a space,
Uplifted seemed Heaven's everlasting door,

And I indeed the darling of Thy grace.
But, in some dozen changes of the moon,
A bitter mockery seemed Thy bitter boon.
The broken pinion was no longer
Again, indeed, I woke
Under so dread a stroke
That all the strength it left within my heart
Was just to ache and turn, and then to turn and ache,
And some weak sign of war unceasingly to make.
And here I lie,
With no one near to mark,
Thrusting Hell's phantoms feebly in the dark,
And still at point more utterly to die.
O God, how long!
Put forth indeed Thy powerful right hand,
While time is yet,
Or never shall I see the blissful land!
Thus I: then God, in pleasant speech and strong
(Which soon I shall forget):
'The man who, though his fights be all defeats,
Still fights,
Enters at last
The heavenly Jerusalem's rejoicing streets
With glory more, and more triumphant rites
Than always-conquering Joshua's, when his blast
The frighted walls of Jericho down cast;
And, lo, the glad surprise
Of peace beyond surmise,
More than in common saints, for ever in his eyes.'

The Married Lover

Why, having won her, do I woo?
Because her spirit's vestal grace
Provokes me always to pursue,
But, spirit-likes eludes embrace;
Because her womanhood is such
That, as on court-days subjects kiss

The Queen's hand, yet so near a touch
Affirms no mean familiarness;
Nay, rather marks more fair the height
Which can with safety so neglect
To dread, as lower ladies might,
That grace could meet with disrespect;
Thus she with happy favour feeds
Allegiance from a love so high
That thence no false conceit proceeds
Of difference bridged, or state put by;
Because although in act and word
As lowly as a wife can be,
Her manners, when they call me lord,
Remind me 'tis by courtesy;
Not with her least consent of will,
Which would my proud affection hurt,
But by the noble style that still
Imputes an unattained desert;
Because her gay and lofty brows,
When all is won which hope can ask,
Reflect a light of hopeless snows,
That bright in virgin ether bask;
Because, though free of the outer court
I am, this Temple keeps its shrine
Sacred to Heaven; because, in short,
She's not and never can be mine.

The Toys

My little Son, who looked from thoughtful eyes
And moved and spoke in quiet grown-up wise,
Having my law the seventh time disobeyed,
I struck him, and dismissed
With hard words and unkissed,
His Mother, who was patient, being dead.
Then, fearing lest his grief should hinder sleep,
I visited his bed,
But found him slumbering deep,

With darkened eyelids, and their lashes
From his late sobbing wet.
And I, with moan,
Kissing away his tears, left others of my own;
For, on a table drawn beside his head,
He had put, within his reach,
A box of counters and a red-veined stone,
A piece of glass abraded by the beach.
And six or seven shells,
A bottle with bluebells,
And two French copper coins, ranged there with careful art,
To comfort his sad heart.
So when that night I prayed
To God, I wept, and said:
Ah, when at last we lie with tranced breath,
Not vexing Thee in death,
And Thou rememberest of what toys
We made our joys,
How weakly understood
Thy great commanded good,
Then, fatherly not less
Than I whom Thou hast moulded from the clay,
Thou'lt leave Thy wrath, and say,
'I will be sorry for their childishness.'

Regina Caeli (Queen of Heaven)

Say, did his sisters wonder what could Joseph see
In a mild, silent little Maid like thee?
And was it awful, in that narrow house,
With God for Babe and Spouse?
Nay, like thy simple, female sort, each one
Apt to find Him in Husband and in Son,
Nothing to thee came strange in this.
Thy wonder was but wondrous bliss:
Wondrous, for, though
True Virgin lives not but does know,
(Howbeit none ever yet confessed,)

That God lies really in her breast,
Of thine He made His special nest!
And so
All mothers worship little feet
And kiss the very ground they've trod;
But, ah, thy little Baby sweet,
Who was indeed thy God!

Magna est Veritas (Great is the Truth)

Here, in this little Bay,
Full of tumultuous life and great repose,
Where, twice a day,
The purposeless, glad ocean comes and goes,
Under high cliffs, and far from the huge town,
I sit me down.
For want of me the world's course will not fail:
When all its work is done, the lie shall rot;
The truth is great, and shall prevail,
When none cares whether it prevail or not.

Pain

O, Pain, Love's mystery,
Close next of kin
To joy and heart's delight,
Low Pleasure's opposite,
Choice food of sanctity
And medicine of sin,
Angel, whom even they that will pursue
Pleasure with hell's whole gust
Find that they must
Perversely woo,
My lips, thy live coal touching, speak thee true.
Thou sear'st my flesh, O Pain,
But brand'st for arduous peace my languid brain,
And bright'nest my dull view,
Till I, for blessing, blessing give again,

And my roused spirit is.
Another fire of bliss,
Wherein I learn
Feelingly how the pangful, purging fire
Shall furiously burn
With joy, not only of assured desire,
But also present joy
Of seeing the life's corruption, stain by stain,
Vanish in the clear heat of Love irate
And, fume by fume, the sick alloy
Of luxury, sloth and hate
Evaporate;
Leaving the man, so dark erewhile,
The mirror merely of God's smile.
Herein, O Pain, abides the praise
For which my song I raise;
But even the bastard good of intermittent ease
How greatly doth it please!
With what repose
The being from its bright exertion glows,
When from thy strenuous storm the senses sweep
Into a little harbour deep
Of rest!

Adelaide Ann Proctor 1825-1864

Thankfulness

My God, I thank Thee Who hast made
The earth so bright;
So full of splendour and of joy,
Beauty and light;
So many glorious things are here,
Noble and right!

I thank Thee, too, that Thou hast made
Joy to abound;

So many gentle thoughts and deeds
Circling us round,
That on the darkest spot of earth
Some love is found.

I thank Thee more that all our joy
Is touched with pain;
That shadows fall on brightest hours;
That thorns remain;
So that earth's bliss may be our guide,
And not our chain.

I thank Thee, Lord, that here our souls,
Though amply blest,
Can never find, although they seek,
A perfect rest;
Nor ever shall, until they lean
On Jesus' breast.

Our Daily Bread

Give us our daily bread,
O God, the bread of strength!
For we have learnt to know
How weak we are at length.
As children we are weak,
As children must be fed –
Give us Thy Grace, O Lord,
To be our daily bread.

Give us our daily bread:
The bitter bread of grief.
We sought earth's poisoned feasts
For pleasure and relief;
We sought her deadly fruits,
But now, O God, instead,
We ask thy healing grief
To be our daily bread.

Give us our daily bread
To cheer our fainting soul;
The feast of comfort, Lord,
And peace, to make us whole:
For we are sick of tears,
The useless tears we shed –
Now give us comfort, Lord,
To be our daily bread.

Give us our daily bread,
The bread of angels, Lord,
For us, so many times,
Broken, betrayed, adored.
His Body and His Blood –
The feast that Jesus spread:
Give Him – our life, our all –
To be our daily bread!

Give Me Thy Heart

With echoing step the worshippers
Departed one by one;
The organ's pealing voice was stilled,
The vesper hymn was done;
The shadows fell from roof and arch,
Dim was the incensed air,
One lamp alone with trembling ray,
Told of the Presence there!

In the dark church she knelt alone;
Her tears were falling fast
'Help, Lord,' she cried, 'the shades of death
Upon my soul are cast!
Have I not shunned the path of sin
And chosen the better part?'
What voice came through the sacred air?
'My child, give me thy heart!'

'For I have loved thee with a love
No mortal heart can show,
A love so deep, My Saints in heaven
Its depths can never know:
When pierced and wounded on the Cross,
Man's sin and doom were Mine,
I loved thee with undying love;
Immortal and divine.'

In awe she listened and the shade
Passed from her soul away;
In low and trembling voice she cried
'Lord, help me to obey!
Break Thou the chains of earth, O Lord,
That bind and hold my heart;
Let it be Thine and Thine alone,
Let none with Thee have part!'

Dante Gabriel Rossetti 1828-1882

Mary's Girlhood (A Study for a Picture)

This is that blessed Mary, pre-elect
God's Virgin. Gone is a great while, and she
Dwelt young in Nazareth of Galilee.
Unto God's will she brought devout respect,
Profound simplicity of intellect,
And supreme patience. From her mother's knee
Faithful and hopeful; wise in charity;
Strong in grave peace; in pity circumspect.
So held she through her girlhood; as it were
An angel-watered lily, that near God
Grows and is quiet. Till, one dawn at home
She woke in her white bed, and had no fear
At all, – yet wept till sunshine, and felt awed
Because the fullness of the time was come.

The Holy Family *(Based upon a painting of Michelangelo)*

Turn not the prophet's page, O Son! He knew
All that Thou hast to suffer, and hath writ.
Not yet Thine hour of knowledge. Infinite
The sorrows that Thy manhood's lot must rue
And dire acquaintance of Thy grief. That clue
The spirits of Thy mournful ministerings
Seek through yon scroll in silence. For these things
The angels have desired to look into.
Still before Eden waves the fiery sword, —
Her Tree of Life unransomed: whose sad Tree
Of Knowledge yet to growth of Calvary
Must yield its Tempter, — Hell the earliest dead
Of Earth resign, — and yet, O Son and Lord,
The seed o' the woman bruise the serpent's head.

Lost Days

The lost days of my life until to-day,
What were they, could I see them on the street
Lie as they fell? Would they be ears of wheat
Sown once for food but trodden into clay?
Or golden coins squandered and still to pay?
Or drops of blood dabbling the guilty feet?
Or such spilt water as in dreams must cheat
The undying throats of Hell, who thirst alway?
I do not see them here; but after death
God knows I know the faces I shall see,
Each one a murdered self, with low last breath.
'I am thyself , — what hast thou done to me?'
'And I — and I — thyself,' (lo! each one saith)
'And thou thyself to all eternity!'

Christina Rossetti 1830-1894

A Bruised Reed Shall He Not Break

I will accept thy will to do and be,
Thy hatred and intolerance of sin,
Thy will at least to love, that burns within
And thirsteth after Me:
So will I render fruitful, blessing still,
The germs and small beginnings in thy heart,
Because thy will cleaves to the better part -
Alas, I cannot will.

Dost not thou will, poor soul? Yet I receive
The inner unseen longings of the soul,
I guide them turning towards Me; I control
And charm hearts till they grieve;
If thou desire, it yet shall come to pass,
Though thou but wish indeed to choose My love;
For I have power in earth and heaven above –
I cannot wish, alas!

What, neither choose nor wish to choose? And yet
I still must strive to win thee and constrain:
For thee I hung upon the Cross in pain,
How then can I forget?
If thou as yet dost neither love, nor hate,
Nor choose, nor wish – resign thyself, be still
Till I infuse love, hatred, longing, will –
I do not deprecate.

After Communion

Why should I call Thee Lord, Who art my God?
Why should I call Thee Friend, who art my Love?
Or King, Who art my very Spouse above?
Or call Thy Sceptre on my heart Thy rod?
Lo, now Thy banner over me is love,
All heaven flies open to me at Thy nod:

For Thou hast lit Thy flame in me a clod,
Made me a nest for dwelling of Thy Dove.
What wilt Thou call me in our home above,
Who now hast called me friend? How will it be
When Thou for good wine settest forth the best?
Now Thou dost bid me come and sup with Thee,
Now Thou dost make me lean upon Thy breast:
How will it be with me in time of love?

A Better Resurrection

I have no wit, no words, no tears;
My heart within me like a stone
Is numbed too much for hopes or fears;
Look right, look left, I dwell alone;
I lift mine eyes, but dimmed with grief
No everlasting hills I see;
My life is in the falling leaf:
O Jesus, quicken me.

My life is like a faded leaf,
My harvest dwindled to a husk;
Truly my life is void and brief
And tedious in the barren dusk;
My life is like a frozen thing,
No bud nor greenness can I see:
Yet rise it shall – the sap of Spring;
O Jesus, rise in me.

My life is like a broken bowl,
A broken bowl that cannot hold
One drop of water for my soul
Or cordial in the searching cold;
Cast in the fire the perished thing,
Melt and remould it, till it be
A royal cup for Him my King:
O Jesus, drink of me.

A Christmas Carol

In the bleak mid-winter
Frosty wind made moan,
Earth stood hard as iron,
Water like a stone,
Snow had fallen, snow on snow,
Snow on snow,
In the bleak mid-winter
Long ago.

Our God, Heaven cannot hold Him
Nor earth sustain;
Heaven and earth shall flee away
When He comes to reign:
In the bleak mid-winter
A stable-place sufficed
The Lord God Almighty
Jesus Christ.

Enough for Him, whom cherubim
Worship night and day,
A breastful of milk
And a mangerful of hay;
Enough for Him whom angels
Fall down before,
The ox and ass and camel
Which adore.

Angels and archangels
May have gathered there,
Cherubim and seraphim
Thronged the air,
But only his mother
In her maiden bliss
Worshipped the Beloved
With a kiss.

What can I give Him,
Poor as I am?
If I were a shepherd
I would bring a lamb,
If I were a Wise Man
I would do my part –
Yet what I can I give Him,
Give my heart.

Good Friday

Am I a stone and not a sheep
That I can stand, O Christ, beneath Thy Cross
To number drop by drop Thy Blood's slow loss
And yet not weep?

Not so those women loved
Who with exceeding grief lamented Thee;
Not so fallen Peter weeping bitterly;
Not so the thief was moved.

Not so the Sun and Moon
Which hid their faces in a starless sky,
A horror of great darkness at broad noon
I, only I.

Yet give not o'er,
But seek Thy Sheep, true Shepherd of the flock,
Greater than Moses, turn and look once more
And smite a rock.

Easter Monday

Out in the rain a world is growing green,
On half the trees quick buds are seen
Where glued-up buds have been.
Out in the rain God's Acre stretches green,
Its harvest quick tho' still unseen:
For there the Life hath been.

If Christ hath died His brethren may well die,
Sing in the gate of death, lay by
This life without a sigh:
For Christ hath died and good it is to die;
In sleep when He lays us by
Then wake without a sigh.

Yea, Christ hath died, yea, Christ is risen again:
Wherefore both life and death grow plain
To us who wax and wane;
For Christ Who rose shall die no more again:
Amen: till He makes all things plain
Let us wax on and wane.

An 'Immurata' Sister

Life flows down to death; we cannot bind
That current that it should not flee:
Life flows down to death, as rivers find
The inevitable sea.

Men work and think, but women feel;
And so (for I'm a woman, I)
And so I should be glad to die,
And cease from impotence of zeal,
And cease from hope, and cease from dread,
And cease from yearnings without gain,
And cease from all this world of pain,
And be at peace among the dead.

Hearts that die, by death renew their youth,
Lightened of this life that doubts and dies;
Silent and contented, while the Truth
Unveiled makes them wise.
Why should I seek and never find
That something which I have not had?
Fair and unutterably sad
The world hath sought time out of mind;

The world hath sought and I have sought –
Ah empty world and empty I!
For we have spent our strength for nought,
And soon it will be time to die.

Sparks fly upward toward their fount of fire,
Kindling, flashing, hovering –
Kindle, flash, my soul; mount higher and higher,
Thou whole burnt-offering!

The Thread of Life

1

The irresponsive silence of the land,
The irresponsive sounding of the sea,
Speak both one message of one sense to me –
'Aloof, aloof, we stand aloof, so stand
Thou too aloof bound with the flawless band
Of inner solitude; we bind not thee;
But who from thy self-chain shall set thee free?
What heart shall touch thy heart? What hand thy hand?'
And I am sometimes proud and sometimes meek,
And sometimes I remember days of old
When fellowship seemed not so far to seek
And all the world and I seemed much less cold,
And at the rainbow's foot lay surely gold,
And hope felt strong and life itself not weak.

2

Thus am I mine own prison. Everything
Around me free and sunny and at ease:
Or if in shadow, in a shade of trees
Which the sun kisses, where the gay birds sing
And where all winds make various murmuring;
Where bees are found, with honey for the bees;
Where sounds are music, and where silences
Are music of an unlike fashioning.
Then gaze I at the merrymaking crew

And smile a moment and a moment sigh
Thinking: Why can I not rejoice with you?
But soon I put the foolish fancy by:
I am not what I have nor what I do;
But what I was I am, I am even I.

3
Therefore myself is that one only thing
I hold to use or waste, to keep or give;
My sole possession every day I live,
And still mine own despite Time's winnowing.
Ever mine own, while moon and seasons bring
From crudeness ripeness mellow and sanative;
Ever mine own, when saints break grave and sing.
And this myself as king unto my King
I give, to Him who gave Himself for me;
Who gives Himself to me, and bids me sing
A sweet new song of His redeemed set free;
He bids me sing, O Death, where is thy sting?
And sing, O grave, where is thy victory?

May Probyn c1840-1890

Soeur Louise de la Misericorde (Louise de la Vallière)

Scourge, and cilice, and feet unshod,
And Office, and fast, and the love of God.
The grille, and the cell, and the sweet vows three,
And the holy habit – for me! for me!

For me, who at first in the state of grace,
Blushed when the great sin looked in my face –

Who housed desire of it unconfessed
In the bosom that once received God for its Guest –

Who, with peril and guilt of it all to me known,
Drank of it, laved in it, made it mine own.

Oh! God of mine, nailed up on the Rood,
Why hast Thou waited? Oh! Kind – oh! Good –

God of my heart, on the bitter Tree
Waiting, when I would not hear of Thee.

My sin loaded the scourge that tore
To pieces the Body that Mary bore –

My sin launched the blows and disgrace
To change and to mar all Thy beautiful Face –

And I, when for ever from pain Thou didst part,
Clove to its centre Thy dear dead heart –

My All! My Jesus! Still can it be,
Thy Heart and the holy habit – for me?

Through the sorrows of Mary Thy Mother, who stood
With the sword in her soul beneath the Rood.

Through the added sorrow her grief brought Thee
Assoil Thou those that have sinned through me...

Chimes! ... and another to-morrow near –
And after tomorrow year on year...

Lord, for such as I used to be
I have given my heart to grief and Thee

To broken sleep, and girdle of iron,
And scourgings to blood, and the flags to lie on –

Wait, wait but for them as for me Thou didst wait,
Who came unwilling, and came so late –

Oh! Kind – oh! Gentle – I chose not Thee –
My Jesus, why hast Thou chosen me?

Chimes ... and the long night going its way
Till the next chime bringeth another day –

Penance, and fast, and the feet unshod,
And a living death, and the love of God.

A Christmas Carol

Lacking samite and sable,
Lacking silver and gold,
The Prince Jesus in the poor stable
Slept, and was three hours old.

As doves by the fair water,
Mary, not touched of sin,
Sat by Him, the King's daughter
All glorious within.

A lily without one stain, a
Star where no spot hath room –
Ave, gratia plena,
Virgo Virginum. [1]

Clad not in pearl-sewn vesture,
Clad not in cramoisie,
She hath hushed, she hath cradled to rest, her
God the first time on her knee.

Where is one to adore Him?
The ox hath dumbly confessed,
With the ass, meek kneeling before Him,
'*Et homo factus est.*' [2]

Not throned on ivory or cedar,
Not crowned with a Queen's crown,
At her breast it is Mary shall feed her
Maker, from Heaven come down.

The trees in Paradise blossom
Sudden, and its bells chime –
She giveth Him, held to her bosom,
Her immaculate milk the first time.

The night with wings of angels
Was alight, and its snow-packed ways
Sweet made (say the Evangels)
With the noise of their virelays.

Quem vidistis, pastores?[3]
Why go ye feet unshod?
Wot ye within yon door is[4]
Mary, the Mother of God?

No smoke of spice ascending
There – no roses are piled –
But, choicer than all balms blending,
There Mary hath kissed her Child.

Dilectus meus mihi et ego illi –[5]
Cold small cheek against her cheek,
He sleepeth, three hours old.

1. Hail, full of grace, maid of maidens. 2. And he was made man. 3. What have
you seen, shepherds?   4. Wot = know.   5. *Dilectus meus mihi et ego illi-* =
Beloved child of mine, and I of Him

Wilfred Scawen Blunt 1840-1922

The Sinner Saint

If I have since done evil in my life,
I was not born for evil. This I know.
My soul was a thing pure from sensual strife.
No vice of the blood foredoomed me to this woe.
I did not love corruption. Beauty, truth,
Justice, compassion, peace with God and man,
These were my laws, the instincts of my youth,
And hold me still, conceal it as I can.
I did not love corruption, nor do love.
I find it ill to hate and ill to grieve.
Nature designed me for a life above
The mere discordant dreams in which I live.

If I now go a beggar on the Earth,
I was a saint of Heaven by right of birth.

How Shall I Build?

How shall I build my temple to the Lord,
Unworthy I, who am thus foul of heart?
How shall I worship who no traitor word
Know but of love to play a suppliant's part?
How shall I pray, whose soul is as a mart,
For thoughts unclean, whose tongue is as a sword
Even for those it loves, to wound and smart?
Behold how little I can help Thee, Lord.

The Temple I would build should be all white,
Each stone the record of a blameless day;
The souls that entered there should walk in light,
Clothed in high chastity and wisely gay.
Lord, here is darkness. Yet this heart unwise,
Bruised in Thy service, take in sacrifice.

Alice Meynell 1847-1922

San Lorenzo's Mother

I had not seen my son's dear face
(He chose the cloister by God's grace)
Since it had come to full flower-time.
I hardly guessed at its perfect prime,
That folded flower of his dear face.

Mine eyes were veiled by mists of tears
When on a day in many years
One of his Order came. I thrilled,
Facing, I thought, that face fulfilled.
I doubted, for my mists of tears.

His blessing be with me for ever!
My hope and doubt were hard to sever.
That altered face, those holy weeds.

I filled his wallet and kissed his beads,
And lost his echoing feet for ever.

If to my son my alms were given
I know not, and I wait for Heaven.
He did not plead for child of mine,
But for another Child divine,
And unto Him it was surely given.

There is One alone Who cannot change;
Dreams are we, shadows, visions strange;
And all I give is given to One.
I might mistake my dearest son,
But never the Son Who cannot change.

In Portugal, 1912

And will they cast the altars down,
Scatter the chalice, crush the bread?
In field, in village, and in town
He hides an unregarded head;

Waits in the corn-lands far and near,
Bright in His sun, dark in His frost,
Sweet in the vine, ripe in the ear –
Lonely unconsecrated Host.

In ambush at the merry board
The Victim lurks unsacrificed;
The mill conceals the harvest's Lord,
The wine-press holds the unbidden Christ.

Renouncement

I must not think of thee; and, tired yet strong,
I shun the thought that lurks in all delight –
The thought of thee – and in the blue Heaven's height,
And in the sweetest passage of a song.
Oh, just beyond the fairest thoughts that throng
This breast, the thought of thee waits, hidden yet bright;

Yet it must never, never come in sight;
I must stop short of thee the whole day long.

But when sleep comes to close each difficult day,
When night gives pause to the long watch I keep,
And all my bonds I needs must loose apart,
Must doff my will as raiment laid away –
With the first dream that comes with the first sleep
I run, I run, I am gathered to thy heart.

A General Communion

I saw the throng, so deeply separate,
Fed at one only board –
The devout people, moved, intent, elate,
And the devoted Lord.

Oh struck apart! Not side from human side,
But soul from human soul,
As each asunder absorbed the multiplied,
The ever unparted whole.

I saw this people as a field of flowers,
Each grown at such a price
The sum of unimaginable powers
Did no more than suffice.

A thousand single central daisies they,
A thousand of the one;
For each, the entire monopoly of day,
For each, the whole of the devoted sun.

Maternity

One wept whose only child was dead,
New-born, ten years ago.
'Weep not; he is in bliss,' they said.
She answered, 'Even so.
Ten years ago was born in pain

A child, not now forlorn.
But oh, ten years ago, in vain
A mother, a mother was born.'

The Young Neophyte

Who knows what days I answer for to-day?
Giving the bud I give the flower. I bow
This yet unfaded and a faded brow
Bending these knees and feeble knees, I pray.
Thoughts yet unripe in me I bend one way,
Give one repose to pain I know not now,
One check to joy that comes, I guess not how.
I dedicate my fields when spring is grey.

O rash! (I smile) to pledge my hidden wheat.
I fold today at altars far apart
Hands trembling with what toils? In their retreat
I seal my love to-be, my folded art.
I light the tapers at my head and feet,
And lay the crucifix on this silent heart.

Christ in the Universe

With this ambiguous earth
His dealings have been told us. These abide:
The signal to a maid, the human birth,
The lesson, and the young man crucified.

But not a star of all
The innumerable host of stars has heard
How He administered this terrestrial ball.
Our race have kept their Lord's entrusted Word.

Of His earth-visiting feet
None knows the secret, cherished, perilous,
The terrible, shamefast, frightened, whispered, sweet,
Heart-shattering secret of His way with us.

No planet knows that this
Our wayside, carrying land and wave,
Love and life multiplied, and pain and bliss,
Bears, as chief treasure, one forsaken grave.

Nor, in our little day,
May His devices with the heavens be guessed,
His pilgrimage to thread the Milky Way,
Or His bestowals there be manifest.

But, in the eternities
Doubtless we shall compare together, hear
A million alien Gospels, in what guise
He trod the Pleiades, the Lyre, the Bear.

Oh, be prepared, my soul!
To read the inconceivable, to scan
The million forms of God those stars unroll
When, in our turn, we show to them a Man.

Thoughts in Separation

We never meet; yet we meet day by day
Upon those hills of life, dim and immense –
The good we love, and sleep, our innocence.
O hills of life, high hills! And, higher than they,
Our guardian spirits meet at prayer and play.
Beyond pain, joy, and hope, and long suspense,
Above the summits of our souls, far hence,
An angel meets an angel on the way.

Beyond all good I ever believed of thee,
Or thou of me, these always love and live.
And though I fail of thy ideal of me,
My angel falls not short. They greet each other.
Who knows, they may exchange the kiss we give
Thou to thy crucifix, I to my mother.

The Lady Poverty

The Lady Poverty was fair:
But she has lost her looks of late,
With change of times and change of air.
Ah slattern! She neglects her hair,
Her gown, her shoes; she keeps no state
As once when her pure feet were bare.

Or – almost worse, if worse can be –
She scolds in parlours, dusts and trims,
Watches and counts. O is this she
Whom Francis met, whose step was free,
Who with Obedience carolled hymns,
In Umbria walked with Chastity?

Where is her ladyhood? Not here,
Not among modern kinds of men;
But in the stony fields, where clear
Through the thin trees the skies appear,
In delicate spare soil and fen,
And slender landscape and austere.

'I am the Way'

Thou art the Way.
Hadst Thou been nothing but the goal,
I cannot say
If Thou hadst ever met my soul.

I cannot see –
I, child of process – if there lies
An end for me,
Full of repose, full of replies.

I'll not reproach
The road that winds, my feet that err.
Access, Approach
Art Thou, Time, Way, and Wayfarer.

The Unknown God

One of the crowd went up,
And knelt before the Paten and the Cup,
Received the Lord, returned in peace, and prayed
Close to my side. Then in my heart I said:

'O Christ, in this man's life –
This stranger who is Thine – in all his strife,
All his felicity, his good and ill,
In the assaulted stronghold of his will,

I do confess Thee here,
Alive within this life; I know Thee near
Within this lonely conscience, closed away
Within this brother's solitary day.

Christ in his unknown heart,
His intellect unknown – this love, this art,
This battle and this peace, this destiny
That I shall never know – look upon me!

Christ in his numbered breath,
Christ in his beating heart and in his death,
Christ in his mystery! From that secret place
And from that separate dwelling, give me grace!'

The Courts – A Figure of the Epiphany

The poet's imageries are noble ways,
Approaches to a plot, an open shrine,
Their splendours, colours, avenues, arrays,
Their courts that run with wine;

Beautiful similes, 'fair and flagrant things,'
Enriched, enamouring, – raptures, metaphors
Enhancing life, are paths for pilgrim kings
Made free of golden doors.

And yet the open heavenward plot, with dew,
Ultimate poetry, enclosed, enskied,
(Albeit such ceremonies lead thereto)
Stands on the yonder side.

Plain, behind oracles, it is; and past
All symbols, simple; perfect, heavenly-wild,
The song some loaded poets reach at last-
The kings that found a Child.

Digby Macworth Dolben 1848-1867

Prayer

From falsehood and error,
From darkness and terror,
From all that is evil,
From the power of the devil,
From the fire and the doom,
From the judgement to come –
Sweet Jesu, deliver
Thy servants forever.

Flowers at the Altar

1
Tell us, tell us, holy shepherds,
What at Bethlehem you saw. –
'Very God of Very God
Asleep amid the straw.'

Tell us, tell us, all ye faithful,
What this morning came to pass
At the awful elevation
In the Canon of the Mass. –

'Very God, of Very God,
By whom the worlds were made,
In silence and in helplessness
Upon the Altar laid.'

Tell us, tell us, wondrous Jesu,
What has drawn Thee from above
To the manger and the Altar.
All the silence answers – Love.

2
Through the roaring streets of London
Thou art passing, hidden Lord,
Uncreated, consubstantial,
In the seventh Heaven adored.

As of old the ever-Virgin
Through unconscious Bethlehem
Bore Thee, not in glad procession,
Jewelled robe and diadem;

Not in pomp and not in power,
Onward to Nativity,
Shined but in the tabernacle
Of her sweet Virginity.

Still thou goest by in silence,
Still the world cannot receive,
Still the poor and weak and weary
Only, worship and believe.

Francis Thompson 1859-1907

The Passion of Mary: Verses in Passion-Tide

O Lady Mary, thy bright crown
Is no mere crown of majesty;
For with the reflex of His own
Resplendent thorns Christ circled thee.

The red rose of this Passion-tide
Doth take a deeper hue from thee,
In the five wounds of Jesus dyed,
And in thy bleeding thoughts, Mary!

214

The soldier struck a triple stroke,
That smote thy Jesus on the tree:
He broke the Hearts of Hearts, and broke
The Saint's and Mother's hearts in thee.

Thy Son went up the angels' ways,
His passion ended; but, ah me!
Thou found'st the road of further days
A longer way of Calvary;

On the hard cross of hope deferred
Thou hung'st in loving agony,
Until the mortal-dreaded word
Which chills *our* mirth, spake mirth to thee.

The angel Death from this cold tomb
Of life did roll the stone away;
And He thou barest in thy womb
Caught thee at last unto the day,
Before the living throne of whom
The Lights of Heaven burning pray.

To a Snowflake

What heart could have thought you? –
Past our devisal
(O filigree petal!)
Fashioned so purely,
Fragilely, surely,
From what Paradisal
Imagineless metal,
Too costly for cost?
Who hammered you, wrought you,
From argentine vapour? –
'God was my shaper.
Passing surmisal,
He hammered, He wrought me,
From curled silver vapour,
To lust of His mind: –

Thou could'st not have thought me!
So purely, so palely,
Tinily, surely,
Mightily, frailly,
Insculped and embossed,
With His hammer of wind,
And His graver of frost.'

'In No Strange Land' (The Kingdom of God is Within You)

O world invisible, we view thee,
O world intangible, we touch thee,
O world unknowable, we know thee,
Inapprehensible, we clutch thee!

Does the fish soar to find the ocean,
The eagle plunge to find the air –
That we ask of the stars in motion
If they have rumour of thee there?

Not where the wheeling systems darken,
And our benumbed conceiving soars!
The drift of pinions, would we hearken,
Beats at our own clay-shuttered doors.

The angels keep their ancient places; –
Turn but a stone, and start a wing!
'Tis ye, 'tis your estranged faces,
That miss the many-splendoured thing.

But (when so sad thou canst not sadder)
Cry; and upon thy so sore loss
Shall shine the traffic of Jacob's ladder
Pitched betwixt Heaven and Charing Cross.

Yea, in the night, my soul, my daughter,
Cry – clinging Heaven by the hems;
And lo, Christ walking on the water
Not of Gennesareth but Thames!

The Hound of Heaven

I fled Him, down the nights and down the days;
I fled Him, down the arches of the years;
I fled Him, down the labyrinthine ways
Of my own mind; and in the midst of tears
I hid from Him, and under running laughter.
Up vistaed hopes I sped;
And shot, precipitated,
Adown Titanic glooms of chasmed fears,
From those strong Feet that followed, followed after.
But with unhurrying chase,
And unperturbed pace,
Deliberate speed, majestic instancy,
They beat – and a Voice beat
More instant than the Feet –
'All things betray thee, who betrayest Me.'

I pleaded, outlaw-wise,
By many a hearted casement, curtained red,
Trellised with intertwining charities;
(For, though I knew His love who followed,
Yet was I sore adread
Lest, having Him, I must have naught beside).
But, if one little casement parted wide,
The gust of His approach would clash it to.
Fear wist not to evade, as Love wist to pursue.
Across the margent of the world I fled,
And troubled the gold gateway of the stars,
Smiting for shelter on their clanged bars;
Fretted to dulcet jars
And silvern chatter the pale ports o' the moon.
I said to Dawn, Be sudden; to Eve, Be soon;
With thy young skiey blossoms heap me over
From his tremendous Lover!
Float thy vague veil about me, lest He see!
I tempted all His servitors, but to find
My own betrayal in their constancy,

In faith to Him their fickleness to me,
Their traitorous trueness, and their loyal deceit.
To all swift things for swiftness did I sue;
Clung to the whistling mane of every wind.
But whether they swept, smoothly fleet,
The long savannahs of the blue;
Or whether, Thunder-driven,
They clanged his chariot 'thwart a heaven
Plashy with flying lightnings round the spurn o' their feet:—
Fear wist not to evade as Love wist to pursue.
Still with unhurrying chase,
And unperturbed pace,
Deliberate speed, majestic instancy,
Came on the following Feet,
And a Voice above their beat —
'Naught shelters thee, who wilt not shelter Me.'

I sought no more that after which I strayed
In face of man or maid;
But still within the little children's eyes
Seems something, something that replies:
They at least are for me, surely for me!
I turned me to them very wistfully;
But just as their young eyes grew sudden fair
With dawning answers there,
Their angel plucked them from me by the hair.
'Come then, ye other children, Nature's — share
With me' (said I) 'your delicate fellowship;
Let me greet you lip to lip,
Let me twine with you caresses,
Wantoning
With our Lady-Mother's vagrant tresses,
Banqueting
With her in her wind-walled palace,
Underneath her azured dais,
Quaffing, as your taintless way is,
From a chalice

Lucent-weeping out of the dayspring.'
So it was done:
I in their delicate fellowship was one –
Drew the bolt of Nature's secrecies.
I knew all the swift importings
On the wilful face of skies;
I knew how the clouds arise
Spumed of the wild sea-snortings;
All that's born or dies
Rose and drooped with; made them shapers
Of mine own moods, or wailful or divine –
With them joyed and was bereaven.
I was heavy with the even,
When she lit her glimmering tapers
Round the day's dead sanctities.
I laughed in the morning's eyes.
I triumphed and I saddened with all weather,
Heaven and I wept together,
And its sweet tears were salt with mortal mine;
Against the red throb of its sunset-heart
I laid my own to beat,
And share commingling heat;
But not by that, by that, was eased my human smart.
In vain my tears were wet on Heaven's grey cheek.
For ah! We know not what each other says,
These things and I; in sound *I* speak –
Their sound is but their stir, they speak by silences.
Nature, poor stepdame, cannot slake my drought;
Let her, if she would owe me,
Drop yon blue bosom-veil of sky, and show me
The breasts o' her tenderness:
Never did any milk of hers once bless
My thirsting mouth.
Nigh and nigh draws the chase,
With unperturbed pace,
Deliberate speed, majestic instancy;
And past those noised feet –

A Voice comes yet more fleet –
'Lo! Naught contents thee, who content'st not Me.'

Naked I wait Thy love's uplifted stroke!
My harness piece by piece Thou hast hewn from me,
And smitten me to my knee;
I am defenceless utterly.
I slept, methinks, and woke,
And, slowly gazing, find me stripped in sleep.
In the rash lustihead of my young powers,
I shook the pillaring hours
And pulled my life upon me; grimed with smears,
I stand amid the dust o' the mounded years –
My mangled youth lies dead beneath the heap.
My days have crackled and gone up in smoke,
Have puffed and burst as sun-starts on a stream.
Yea, faileth now even dream
The dreamer, and the lute the lutanist;
Even the linked fantasies, in whose blossomy twist
I swung the earth a trinket at my wrist,
Are yielding; cords of all too weak account
For earth with heavy griefs so overplussed.
Ah! Is Thy love indeed
A weed, albeit an amaranthine weed,
Suffering no flowers except its own to mount?
Ah! Must –
Designer infinite!
Ah! Must Thou char the wood ere Thou canst limn with it?
My freshness spent its wavering shower i'the dust;
And now my heart is as a broken fount,
Wherein tear-drippings stagnate, spilt down ever
From the dank thoughts that shiver
Upon the sighful branches of my mind.
Such is; what is to be?
The pulp, so bitter, how shall taste the rind?
I dimly guess what Time in mists confounds;
Yet ever and anon a trumpet sounds

From the hid battlements of Eternity;
Those shaken mists a space unsettle, then
Round the half-glimpsed turrets slowly wash again
But not ere him who summoneth
I first have seen, enwound
With glooming robes purpureal, cypress-crowned;
His name I know, and what his trumpet saith.
Whether man's heart or life it be which yields
Thee harvest, must Thy harvest fields
Be dunged with rotten death?

Now of that long pursuit
Comes on at hand the bruit;
That Voice is round me like a bursting sea:
'And is thy earth so marred,
Shattered in shard on shard?
Lo! All things fly thee, for thou fliest Me!
Strange, piteous, futile thing!
Wherefore should any set thee love apart?
Seeing none but I makes much of naught' (He said)
'And human love needs human meriting:
How hast thou merited –
Of all man's clotted clay the dingiest clot?
Alack, thou knowest not
How little worthy of any love thou art!
Whom wilt thou find to love ignoble thee
Save Me, save only Me?
All which I took from thee I did but take,
Not for thy harms,
But just that thou might'st seek it in My arms.
All which thy child's mistake
Fancies as lost, I have stored for thee at home:
Rise, clasp My hand, and come!'

Halts by me that footfall:
Is my gloom, after all,
Shade of His hand, outstretched caressingly?
'Ah, fondest, blindest, weakest,

I am He Whom thou seekest!
Thou drawest love from thee, who drawest Me.'

To the English Martyrs (extract)

Rain, rain on Tyburn tree,[1]
Red rain a-falling;
Dew, dew on Tyburn tree,
Red dew on Tyburn tree,
And the swart bird a-calling.
The shadow lies on England now
Of the deathly-fruited bough:
Cold and black with malison
Lies between the land and sun;
Putting out the sun, the bough
Shades England now!

The troubled heavens do wan with care,
And burthened with the earth's despair
Shiver a-cold; the starved heaven
Has want, with wanting man bereaven.
Blest fruit of the unblest bough,
Aid the land that smote you, now!
That feels the sentence and the curse
Ye died if so ye might reverse.
When God was stolen from out man's mouth,
Stolen was the bread; then hunger and drouth
Went to and fro; began the wail,
Struck root the poor-house and the jail.
Ere cut the dykes, let through that flood,
Ye writ the protest with your blood;
Against this night – wherein our breath
Withers, and the toiled heart perisheth –
Entered the *caveat* of your death.
Christ in the form of His true Bride,
Again hung pierced and crucified,
And groaned, 'I thirst!' Not still ye stood –
Ye had your hearts, ye had your blood;

And pouring out the eager cup –
'The wine is weak, yet, Lord Christ, sup!'
Ah, blest! Who bathed the parched Vine
With richer than His Cana-wine,
And heard, your most sharp supper past:
'Ye kept the best wine to the last!'
Ah, happy who
That sequestered secret knew,
How sweeter than bee-haunted dells,
The blosmy blood of martyrs smells!
Who did upon the scaffold's bed,
The ceremonial steel between you, wed
With God's grave proxy, high and reverend Death;
Or felt about your neck, sweetly,
(While the dull horde
Saw but the unrelenting cord)
The Bridegroom's arm, and that long kiss
That kissed away your breath, and claimed you His.
You did, with thrift of holy gain,
Unvenoming the sting of pain,
Hive its sharp heather-honey. Ye
Had sentience of the mystery
To make Abaddon's hooked wings
Buoy you up to starry things;
Pain of heart, and pain of sense,
Pain the scourge, ye taught to cleanse;
Pain the loss became possessing;
Pain the curse was pain the blessing.
Chains, rack, hunger, solitude – these,
Which did your soul from earth release,
Left it free to rush upon
And merge in its compulsive Sun.
Desolated, bruised, forsaken,
Nothing taking, all things taken,
Lacerated and tormented,
The stifled soul, in naught contented,
On all hands straitened, cribbed, denied,

Can but fetch breath o' the Godward side.
Oh, to me, give but to me
That flower of felicity,
Which on your topmost spirit ware
The difficult and snowy air
Of high refusal! And the heat
Of central love which fed with sweet
And holy fire i' the frozen sod
Roots that ta'en hold on God.

1. Tyburn Tree: popular name of the gallows at Tyburn in London where many
of the English martyrs were executed.

Louise Imogen Guiney 1861-1920

Two Christmas Carols

1

Vines branching stilly
Shade the open door,
In the house of Zion's Lily,
Cleanly and poor.
Oh, brighter than wild laurel
The Babe bounds in her hand,
The King, who for apparel
Hath but a swaddling-band,
And sees her heavenlier smiling than stars in His command!

Soon, mystic changes
Part Him from her breast,
Yet there awhile He ranges
Gardens of rest:
Yea, she the first to ponder
Our ransom and recall,
Awhile may rock Him under
Her young curls' fall,
Against that only sinless love-loyal heart of all.

What shall inure Him
Unto the deadly dream,
When the Tetrarch shall abjure Him,
The thief blaspheme,
And scribe and soldier jostle
About the shameful tree,
And even an Apostle
Demand to touch and see? –
But she hath kissed her Flower where the
Wounds are to be.

2

Three without slumber ride from afar,
Fain of the roads where palaces are;
All by a shed as they ride in a row,
'Here!' is the cry of their vanishing Star.

First doth a greybeard glittering fine,
Look on Messiah in slant moonshine:
'This have I bought for Thee!' Vainly: for lo,
Shut like a fern is the young hand divine.

Next doth a magician, mantled and tall,
Bow to the Ruler that reigns from a stall:
'This have I sought for Thee!' Though it be rare,
Loathe little fingers are letting it fall.

Last doth a stripling, bare in his pride,
Kneel by the Lover as if to abide:
'This have I wrought for Thee!' Answer him there
Laugh of a Child, and His arms opened wide.

Triste Noel

The ox he openeth wide the door,
And from the snow he calls her in,
And he hath seen her smile therefore,
Our Lady without sin.

Now soon from sleep
A star shall leap,
And soon arrive both king and hind
Amen, Amen:
But O the place could I but find!

The Ox hath hushed his voice and bent
True eyes of pity ere the mow,
And on his lovely neck, forspent,
The blessed lays her brow.
Around her feet,
Full warm and sweet
His bowery breath doth meekly smell:
Amen, Amen:
But sore I am with vain travel!

The ox is host in Judah stall
And host of more than only one,
For close she gathereth withal
Our Lord her little son.
Glad hind and king
Their gift may bring,
But would tonight my tears were there
Amen, Amen:
Between her bosom and His hair!

The Kings

A man said unto his Angel:
'My spirits are fallen low,
And I cannot carry this battle:
O brother! Where might I go?

The terrible Kings are on me
With spears that are deadly bright;
Against me so from the cradle
Do fate and my fathers fight.'

Then said to the man his Angel:
'Thou wavering witless soul,
Back to the ranks! What matter
To win or to lose the whole,

As judged by the little judges
Who hearken not well, nor see?
Not thus, by the outer issue,
The Wise shall interpret thee.

Thy will is the sovereign measure
And only event of things:
The puniest heart defying,
Were stronger than all these Kings.

Though out of the past they gather,
Mind's Doubt, and Bodily Pain,
And pallid Thirst of the Spirit
That is kin to the other twain,

And Grief, in a cloud of banners,
And ringletted Vain Desires,
And Vice, with spoils upon him
Of thee and thy beaten sires:–

While Kings of Eternal evil
Yet darken the hills about,
Thy part is with broken sabre
To rise on the last redoubt;

To fear not sensible failure,
Nor covet the game at all,
But fighting, fighting, fighting,
Die, driven against the wall.'

Katherine Tynan Hinkson 1861-1931

Of an Orchard

God is an orchard, the saint saith,
To meditate on life and death,
With a cool well, a hive of bees,
A hermit's grot beneath the trees.

Good is an orchard: very good,
Though one should wear no monkish hood.
Right good when Spring awakes her flute,
And good in yellowing time of fruit.

Very good in the grass to lie
And see the network 'gainst the sky,
A living lace of blue and green,
And boughs that let the gold between.

The bees are types of souls that dwell
With honey in a quiet cell;
The ripe fruit figures goldenly
The soul's perfection in God's eye.

Prayer and praise in a country home,
Honey and fruit; a man might come,
Fed on such meats, to walk abroad,
And in his orchard talk with God.

The Man of the House

Joseph, honoured from sea to sea,
This is your name that pleases me,
'Man of the House.'

I see you rise at the dawn and light
The fire and blow till the flame is bright.

I see you take the pitcher and carry
The deep well-water for Jesus and Mary.

You knead the corn for the bread so fine,
Gather them grapes from the hanging vine.

There are little feet that are soft and slow,
Follow you whithersoever you go.

There's a little face at your workshop door,
A little one sits down on your floor:

Holds His hands for the shavings curled,
The soft little hands that have made the world.

Mary calls you: the meal is ready:
You swing the Child to your shoulder steady.

I see your quiet smile as you sit
And watch the little Son thrive and eat.

The vine curls by the window space,
The wings of angels cover the face.

Up in the rafters, polished and olden,
There's a dove that broods and his wings are golden.

You who kept them through shine and storm,
A staff, a shelter kindly and warm.

Father of Jesus, husband of Mary,
Hold us your lilies for sanctuary!

Joseph, honoured from sea to sea,
Guard me mine and my own roof-tree,
'Man of the House'!

Mater Dei

She looked to east, she looked to west,
Her eyes, unfathomable, mild,
That saw both worlds, came home to rest –
Home to her own sweet child:
God's golden head was at her breast.

What need to look o'er land and sea?
What could the winged ships bring to her?
What gold or gems of price might be,
Ivory or miniver,
Since God Himself lay on her knee?

What could th'intense blue heaven keep
To draw her eyes and thoughts so high?
All heaven was where her Boy did leap,
Where her foot quietly
Went rocking the dear God asleep.

The angel folk fared up and down
A Jacob's Ladder hung between
Her quiet chamber and God's Town.
She saw unawed, serene;
Since God Himself played by her gown.

The House of the Lord

I would choose to be a doorkeeper
In the House of the Lord
Rather than lords and ladies
In satin on the sward.
To draw the bolts for the white souls
Would be my rich reward:
And I the happy doorkeeper
To the House of the Lord.

Of all who troop in not one comes out
From the House of the Lord,
Those who have won from sin and death,
From age and grief abhorred.
There is more room within its courts
Than palaces afford;
So great it is and spacious
In the House of the Lord.

They come with shining faces
To the House of the Lord;
The broken hearts and weary
That life has racked and scored:
They come hurrying and singing
To sit down at His board,
They are young and they are joyful
In the House of the Lord.

There are lilies and daisies
In the House of the Lord.
The lover finds his lover
With a long, long regard.
The mothers find the children.
Strayed from their watch and ward,
O the meetings and the greetings
In the House of the Lord!

I would be a humble doorkeeper
In the House of the Lord,
Where the courts are white and shining
In the Light of the Word.
When the saved souls come trooping
For the gates to be unbarred.
O blessed is the doorkeeper
In the House of the Lord!

Fr John Gray 1866-1934

Balladare

The sheltered garden sleeps among the tall
Black poplars which grow round it, next the wall.
The wall is very high, green grown on red.
All is within, white convent, chapel, all.

Slight supper past, the evening office said,
Gardening tools locked up, the poultry fed,
Little is done but lazy chaplets told,
Weeds plucked, and garden calvaries visited.

Some pace and stitch; some read in little, old,
Worn, heavily bound missals, which they hold
With both red hands, where lawns are foiled with flowers
Lily and Ladybell and Marygold.

This is the least unhushed evening hours,
When blessed peace best wears its dearest dowers;
Quietly grouped are nuns and novices;
Two tiny ladies play with battledores.

Drunk with the blows, unsteady with the whizz
Of whirling flight, the shuttlecock seems, is
Alive and fluttering at each new shock.
Sisters are drawing close by twos and threes.

Asthmatic mother, as the shuttlecock
Flies straight at her, allows herself to knock
It onward with her leaf fan, muttering,
Half as excuse: ''Tis nearly nine o'clock.'

What better warrant for a foolish thing:
With swift inventiveness the sisters bring
Whatever light thing strikes; old copybooks
Fulfil the purpose well. Such fluttering

Within the convent walls the sober rooks
Who live among the poplar branches – Sooks!
Had seldom seen. Now all the place prevails
With cries and laughter to its furthest nooks.

The novices and nuns catch up their tails,
Better to bustle, darting till their veils
Float back and tangle in the merry fuss,
Till sombre weeds swell out like lusty sails.

'Peace', croaks the mother, 'Peace, the angelus!'

Lord, if Thou art not Present

Lord, if Thou art not present, where shall I
Seek Thee the absent? If Thou art everywhere,
How is it that I do not see Thee nigh?

Thou dwellest in a light remote and fair.
How can I reach that light, Lord? I beseech
Thee, teach my seeking, and Thyself declare –

Thyself the sought to me. Unless Thou teach
Me, Lord, I cannot seek; nor can I find
Thee, if Thou wilt not come within my reach.

Lord, let me seek, with sturdy heart and mind,
In passion of desire and longingly.
Let me desire Thee, seeking Thee; and find...

Loving Thee, find Thee; love Thee, finding Thee.

Lionel Johnson 1867-1902

The Dark Angel

Dark Angel, with thine aching lust
To rid the world of penitence:
Malicious Angel, who still dost
My soul such subtle violence!

Because of thee, no thought, no thing,
Abides for me undesecrate:
Dark Angel, ever on the wing,
Who never reachest me too late!

When music sounds, then changest thou
Its silvery to a sultry fire:
Nor will thine envious heart allow
Delight untortured by desire.

Through thee, the gracious Muses turn
To Furies, O mine Enemy!
And all the things of beauty burn
With flames of evil ecstasy.

Because of thee, the land of dreams
Becomes a gathering place of fears:
Until tormented slumber seems
One vehemence of useless tears.

When sunlight glows upon the flowers,
Or ripples down the dancing sea:
Thou, with thy troop of passionate powers,
Beleaguerest, bewilderest, me.

Within the breath of autumn woods,
Within the winter silences:
Thy venomous spirit stirs and broods,
O Master of impieties!

The ardour of red flame is thine,
And thine the steely soul of ice:
Thou poisonest the fair design
Of nature, with unfair device.

Apples of ashes, golden bright;
Waters of bitterness, how sweet!
O banquet of a foul delight,
Prepared by thee, dark Paraclete!

Thou art the whisper in the gloom,
The hinting tone, the haunting laugh:
Thou art the adorner of my tomb,
The minstrel of mine epitaph.

I fight thee, in the Holy Name!
Yet, what thou dost, is what God saith:
Tempter! Should I escape thy flame,
Thou wilt have helped my soul from Death:

The second Death, that never dies,
That cannot die, when time is dead:
Live Death, wherein the lost soul cries,
Eternally uncomforted.

Dark Angel, with thine aching lust!
Of two defeats, of two despairs:
Less dread, a change to drifting dust,
Than thine eternity of cares.

Do what thou wilt, thou shalt not so,
Dark Angel! Triumph over me:
Lonely, unto the Lone I go;
Divine, to the Divinity.

The Church of a Dream

Sadly the dead leaves rustle in the whistling wind,
Around the weather-worn, grey church, low down the vale:
The saints in golden vesture shake before the gale;
The glorious windows shake, where still they dwell
        enshrined;
Old saints, by long dead, shrivelled hands, long since
        designed:
There still, although the world autumnal be, and pale,
Still in their golden vesture the old saints prevail;
Alone with Christ, desolate else, left by mankind.

Only one ancient Priest offers the Sacrifice,
Murmuring holy Latin immemorial:
Swaying with tremulous hands
The old censer full of spice,
In grey, sweet incense clouds; blue sweet clouds mystical:
To him, in place of men, for he is old, suffice
Melancholy remembrances and vesperal.

To My Patrons

Thy spear rent Christ, when dead for me He lay:
My sin rends Christ, though never one save He
Perfectly loves me, comforts me. Then pray,
Longinus Saint! The Crucified, for me.

Hard is the holy war, and hard the way:
At rest with ancient victors would I be.
O faith's first glory from our England! Pray,
Saint Alban! To the Lord of Hosts, for me.

Fain would I watch with thee, till morning grey,
Beneath the stars austere: so might I see
Sunrise, and light, and joy, at last. Then pray,
John Baptist Saint! Unto the Christ, for me.

Remembering God's coronation day;
Thorns for His crown; His throne, a Cross: to thee
Heaven's kingdom, dearer was than earth's,
Then pray St Louis! Unto the King of kings, for me.

Thy love loved all things: thy love knew no stay,
But drew the very wild beasts round thy knee.
O lover of the least and lowest! Pray,
St Francis! To the Son of Man, for me.

Bishop of souls in servitude astray,
Who didst for holy service set them free:
Use still thy discipline of love, and pray,
St Charles! Unto the world's High Priest, for me.

Our Lady of the Snows

Far from the world, far from delight,
Distinguishing not day from night;
Vowed to one sacrifice of all
The happy things, that men befall;
Pleading one sacrifice, before
Whom sun and sea and wind adore;
Far from earth's comfort, far away,
We cry to God, we cry and pray
For men, who have the common day.
Dance, merry world! And sing: but we,
Hearing, remember Calvary:
Get gold, and thrive you! But the sun
Once paled; and the centurion
Said: '*This dead man was God's own Son*'.
Think you, we shrink from common toil,
Works of the mart, works of the soil;
That, prisoners of strong despair,
We breathe this melancholy air;
Forgetting the dear calls of race,
And bonds of house, and ties of place;
That, cowards, from the field we turn,

And heavenward, in our weakness, yearn?
Unjust! Unjust! While you despise
Our lonely years, our mournful cries:
You are the happier for our prayer;
The guerdon of our souls, you share.
Not in such feebleness of heart,
We play our solitary part;
Not fugitives of battle, we
Hide from the world, and let things be:
But rather, looking over earth,
Between the bounds of death and birth;
And sad at heart, for sorrow and sin,
We wondered, where might help begin.
And on our wonder came God's choice,
A sudden light, a clarion voice,
Clearing the dark, and sounding clear:
And we obeyed: behold us, here!
In prison bound, but with your chains:
Sufferers, but of alien pains.
Merry the world, and thrives apace,
Each in his customary place:
Sailors upon the carrying sea,
Shepherds upon the pasture lea,
And merchants of the town; and they,
Who march to death, the fighting way;
And there are lovers in the spring,
With those, who dance, and those who sing:
The commonwealth of every day,
Eastward and westward, far away,
Once the sun paled; once cried aloud
The Roman, from beneath the cloud:
'*This day the Son of God is dead!*'
Yet heed men, what the Roman said?
They heed not: we then heed for them,
The mindless of Jerusalem;
Careless, they live and die: but we
Care, in their stead, for Calvary.

O joyous men and women! Strong,
To urge the wheel of life along,
With strenuous arm, and cheerful strain,
And wisdom of laborious brain:
We give our life, our heart, our breath,
That you may live to conquer death;
That, past your tomb, with souls in health,
Joy may be yours, and blessed wealth;
Through vigils of the painful night,
Our spirits with your tempters fight:
For you, for you, we live alone,
Where no joy comes, where cold winds moan:
Nor friends have we, nor have we foes;
Our Queen is of the lonely Snows.
Ah! And sometimes, our prayers between,
Come sudden thoughts of what hath been:
Dreams! And from dreams, once more we fall
To prayer: *'God save, Christ keep, them all.'*
And thou, who knowest not these things,
Hearken, what news our message brings!
Our toils, thy joy of life forgot:
Our lives of prayer forget thee not.

Quisque Suos Manes (What Kind of Spirits are You?)

What have you seen, eyes of strange fire! What have
    you seen,
Far off, how far away! Long since, so long ago!
To fill you with this jewel flame, this frozen glow:
Haunted and hard, still eyes, malignant and serene?
In what wild place of fear, what Pan's wood, have
    you been,
That struck your lustrous rays into a burning snow?
What agonies were yours? What never equalled woe?
Eyes of strange fire, strange eyes of fire! On what
    dread scene?

Smitten and purged, you saw the red deeps of your sin:
You saw there death in life; you will see life in death.
The sunlight shrank away, the moon came wan and thin,
Among the summer trees the sweet winds held their breath.
Now those celestial lights, which you can never win,
Haunt you, and pierce, and blind. The Will of God so saith.

Magic

They wrong with ignorance a royal choice,
Who cavil at my loneliness and labour:
For them, the luring wonder of a voice,
The viol's cry for them, the harp and tabour:
For me divine austerity,
And voices of philosophy.

Ah! Light imaginations, that discern
No passion in the citadel of passion:
Their fancies lie on flowers; but my thoughts turn
To thoughts and things of an eternal fashion:
The majesty and dignity
Of everlasting verity.

Mine is the sultry sunset, when the skies
Tremble with strange, intolerable thunder:
And at the dead of an hushed night, these eyes
Draw down the soaring oracles winged with wonder:
From the four winds they come to me,
The Angels of Eternity.

Men pity me; poor men, who pity me!
Poor, charitable, scornful souls of pity!
I choose laborious loneliness: and ye
Lead Love in triumph through the dancing city:
While death and darkness girdle me,
I grope for immortality.

Ernset Dowson 1867-1900

Vitae Summa Brevis Spem Nos Vetat Incohare Longam. [1]

They are not long, the weeping and the laughter,
Love and desire and hate:
I think they have no portion in us after
We pass the gate.

They are not long, the days of wine and roses
Out of a misty dream
Our path emerges for a while, then closes
Within a dream.

1. The hopes of this life are short, it is not possible to pursue them for long.

Benedictio Domini

Without, the sullen noises of the street!
The voice of London, inarticulate,
Hoarse and blaspheming, surges in to meet
The silent blessing of the Immaculate.

Dark is the church, and dim the worshippers,
Hushed with bowed heads as though by some old spell,
While through the incense-laden air there stirs
The admonition of a silver bell.

Dark is the church, save where the altar stands,
Dressed like a bride, illustrious with light,
Where one old priest exalts with tremulous hands
The one true solace of man's fallen plight.

Strange silence here: without, the sounding street
Heralds the world's swift passage to the fire:
O Benediction, perfect and complete!
When shall men cease to suffer and desire?

Extreme Unction

Upon the eyes, the lips, the feet,
On all the passages of sense,
The atoning oil is spread with sweet
Renewal of lost innocence.

The feet, that lately ran so fast
To meet desire, are soothly sealed;
The eyes, that were so often cast
On vanity, are touched and healed.

From troublous sights and sounds set free;
In such a twilight hour of breath,
Shall one retrace his life, or see,
Through shadows, the true face of death?

Vials of mercy! Sacring oils!
I know not where nor when I come,
Nor through what wanderings and toils,
To crave of you Viaticum.

Yet, when the walls of flesh grow weak,
In such an hour, it well may be,
Through mist and darkness, light will break,
And each anointed sense will see.

Nuns of the Perpetual Adoration

Calm, sad, secure; behind high convent walls,
These watch the sacred lamp, these watch and pray:
And it is one with them when evening falls,
And one with them the cold return of day.

These heed not time; their nights and days they make
Into a long, returning rosary,
Whereon their lives are threaded for Christ's sake:
Meekness and vigilance and chastity.

A vowed patrol, in silent companies,
Life-long they keep before the living Christ:
In the dim church, their prayers and penances
Are fragrant incense to the Sacrificed.

Outside, the world is wild and passionate;
Man's weary laughter and his sick despair
Entreat at their impenetrable gate:
They heed no voices in their dream of prayer.

They saw the glory of the world displayed;
They saw the bitter of it, and the sweet;
They knew the roses of the world should fade,
And be trod under by the hurrying feet.

Therefore they rather put away desire,
And crossed their hands and came to sanctuary;
And veiled their heads and put on coarse attire:
Because their comeliness was vanity.

And there they rest; they have serene insight
Of the illuminating dawn to be:
Mary's sweet Star dispels for them the night,
The proper darkness of humanity.

Calm, sad, secure; with faces worn and mild:
Surely their choice of vigil is the best?
Yea! For our roses fade, the world is wild;
But there, beside the altar, there, is rest.

PART V

The Church in the Modern World 1900-

The arrival of the twentieth century brought new challenges to the Church, as it did to society generally. The confident certainties of the Victorian period were replaced by a more doubtful, questioning tone in most areas of intellectual life. Few great poets of the period wrote much obviously Catholic verse, although Roy Campbell, Michael Ffinch and Caryll Houselander stand comparison with their distinguished predecessors. (Hopkins' poetry was disregarded in his lifetime, and not published until 1918 – which is why it is placed in this section.)

Fr Gerard Manley Hopkins 1844-1889

Heaven-Haven (A nun takes the veil)

> I have desired to go
> Where springs not fail,
> To fields where flies no sharp and sided hail
> And a few lilies blow.
>
> And I have asked to be
> Where no storms come,
> Where the green swell is in the havens dumb,
> And out of the swing of the sea.

God's Grandeur

> The world is charged with the grandeur of God.
> It will flame out, like shining from shook foil;
> It gathers to a greatness, like the ooze of oil
> Crushed. Why do men then now not reck his rod?
> Generations have trod, have trod, have trod;
> And all is seared with trade; bleared, smeared with toil;
> And wears man's smudge and shares man's smell: the soil
> Is bare now, nor can foot feel, being shod.
>
> And for all this, nature is never spent;
> There lives the dearest freshness deep down things;
> And though the last lights off the black West went
> Oh, morning, at the brown brink eastwards, springs –
> Because the Holy Ghost over the bent
> World broods with warm breast and with ah! bright wings.

The Habit of Perfection

> Elected Silence, sing to me
> And beat upon my whorled ear,
> Pipe me to pastures still and be
> The music that I care to hear.

Shape nothing, lips; be lovely-dumb:
It is the shut, the curfew sent
From there where all surrenders come
Which only makes you eloquent.

Be shelled, eyes, with double dark
And find the uncreated light:
This ruck and reel which you remark
Coils, keeps, and teases simple sight.

Palate, the hutch of tasty lust,
Desire not to be rinsed with wine:
The can must be so sweet, the crust
So fresh that come in fasts divine!

Nostrils, your careless breath that spend
Upon the stir and keep of pride,
What relish shall the censers send
Along the sanctuary side!

O feel-of-primrose hands, O feet
That want the yield of plushy sward,
But you shall walk the golden Street
And you unhouse and house the Lord.

And, Poverty, be thou the bride
And now the marriage feast begun,
And lily-coloured clothes provide
Your spouse not laboured-at nor spun.

The Wreck of the Deutschland (Part the First)

(To the happy memory of five Franciscan nuns, exiles by the Falck Laws, drowned between midnight and morning of 7 December 1875.)

1

THOU mastering me
God! Giver of breath and bread;
World's strand, sway of the sea;
Lord of living and dead;
Thou hast bound bones and veins in me, fastened me flesh,
And after it almost unmade, what with dread,
Thy doing: and dost thou touch me afresh?
Over again I feel thy finger and find thee.

2

I did say yes
O at lightning and lashed rod;
Thou heardst me truer than tongue confess
Thy terror, O Christ, O God;
Thou knowest the walls, altar and hour and night:
The swoon of a heart that the sweep and the hurl of
    thee trod
Hard down with a horror of height:
And the midriff astrain with leaning of, laced with fire
    of stress.

3

The frown of his face
Before me, the hurtle of hell
Behind, where, where was a, where was a place?
I whirled out wings that spell
And fled with a fling of the heart to the heart of the Host.
My heart, but you were dovewinged, I can tell,
Carrier-witted, I am bold to boast,
To flash from the flame to the flame then, tower from the
    grace to the grace.

4

I am soft sift
In an hourglass – at the wall
Fast, but mined with a motion, a drift,
And it crowds and it combs to the fall;
I steady as a water in a well, to a poise, to a pane,
But roped with, always, all the way down from the tall
Fells or flanks of the voel, a vein [1]
Of the gospel proffer, a pressure, a principle, Christ's gift.

5

I kiss my hand
To the stars, lovely-asunder
Starlight, wafting him out of it; and
Glow, glory in thunder;
Kiss my hand to the dappled-with-damson west:
Since, tho' he is under the world's splendour and wonder,
His mystery must be instressed, stressed;
For I greet him the days I meet him, and bless when
    I understand.

6

Not out of his bliss
Springs the stress felt
Nor first from heaven (and few know this)
Swings the stroke dealt –
Stroke and a stress that stars and storms deliver,
That guilt is hushed by, hearts are flushed by and melt –
But it rides time like riding a river
(And here the faithful waver, the faithless fable and miss).

7

It dates from day
Of his going in Galilee;
Warm-laid grave of a womb-life grey;
Manger, maiden's knee;
The dense and the driven Passion, and frightful sweat:

Thence the discharge of it, there its swelling to be,
Though felt before, though in high flood yet –
What none would have known of it, only the heart, being
　　hard at bay.

8

Is out with it! Oh,
We lash with the best or worst
Word last! How a lush-kept plush-capped sloe
Will, mouthed to flesh-burst,
Gush! – Flush the man, the being with it, sour or sweet,
Brim, in a flash, full! – Hither then, last or first,
To hero of Calvary, Christ's feet –
Never ask if meaning it, wanting it, warned of it – men go.

9

Be adored among men,
God, three-numbered form;
Wring thy rebel, dogged in den,
Man's malice, with wrecking and storm.
Beyond saying sweet, past telling of tongue,
Thou art lightning and love, I found it, a winter and warm;
Father and fondler of heart thou hast wrung:
Hast thy dark descending and most art merciful then.

10

With an anvil-ding
And with fire in him forge thy will
Or rather, rather then, stealing as Spring
Through him, melt him but master him still:
Whether at once, as once at a crash Paul,
Or as Austin, a lingering-out sweet skill, [2]
Make mercy in all of us, out of us all
Mastery, but be adored, but be adored King.

1. Voel, Welsh for bare mountainside. 2. Austin = St Augustine's slow
conversion, contrasted with that of St Paul.

Carrion Comfort

Not, I'll not, carrion comfort, Despair, not feast on thee;
Not untwist – slack they may be – these last strands of man
In me or, most weary, cry *I can no more.* I can;
Can something, hope, wish day come, not choose not to be.
But ah, but O thou terrible, why wouldst thou rude on me
Thy wring-world right foot rock? Lay a lionlimb against
    me? Scan
With darksome devouring eyes my bruised bones? And fan,
O in turns of tempest, me heaped there; me frantic to avoid
    thee and flee?

Why? That my chaff might fly; my grain lie, sheer and clear.
Nay in all that toil, that coil, since (seems) I kissed the rod,
Hand rather, my heart lo! Lapped strength, stole joy, would
    laugh, cheer.
Cheer whom though? The hero whose heaven-handling
    flung me, foot trod
Me? Or me that fought him? O which one? Is it each one?
    That night, that year
Of now done darkness I wretch lay wrestling with (my
    God!) my God.

Patience

Patience, hard thing! The hard thing but to pray,
But bid for, Patience is! Patience who asks
Wants war, wants wounds; weary his times, his tasks;
To do without, take tosses, and obey.

Rare patience roots in these, and, these away,
Nowhere. Natural heart's ivy, Patience masks
Our ruins of wrecked past purpose. There she basks
Purple eyes and seas of liquid leaves all day.

We hear our hearts grate on themselves: it kills
To bruise them dearer. Yet the rebellious wills
Of us we do bid God bend to him even so.

And where is he who more and more distills
Delicious kindness? – He is patient. Patience fills
His crisp combs, and that comes those ways we know.

Thou Art Indeed Just, Lord

Thou art indeed just, Lord, if I contend
With thee; but, sir, so what I plead is just.
Why do sinners' ways prosper? And why must
Disappointment all I endeavour end?
Wert thou my enemy, O thou my friend,
How wouldst thou worse, I wonder, than thou dost
Defeat, thwart me? Oh, the sots and thralls of lust
Do in spare hours more thrive than I that spend,
Sir, life upon thy cause. See, banks and brakes
Now, leaved how thick! Laced they are again
With fretty chervil, look, and fresh wind shakes
    Them; birds build – but not I build; no, but strain,
Time's eunuch, and not breed one work that wakes.
Mine, O thou lord of life, send my roots rain.

I Wake and Feel the Fell of Dark

I wake and feel the fell of dark, not day.
What hours, O what black hours we have spent
This night! What sights you, heart, saw; ways you went!
And more must, in yet longer light's delay.
With witness I speak this. But where I say
Hours I mean years, mean life. And my lament
Is cries countless, cries like dead letters sent
To dearest him that lives alas! Away.

I am gall, I am heartburn. God's most deep decree
Bitter would have me taste: my taste was me;
Bones built in me, flesh filled, blood brimmed the curse.
Selfyeast of spirit a dull dough sours. I see
The lost are like this, and their scourge to be
As I am mine, their sweating selves; but worse.

Pied Beauty

Glory be to God for dappled things –
For skies of couple-colour as a brinded cow;
For rose-moles in all stipple upon trout that swim;
Fresh-firecoal chestnut-falls; finches' wings;
Landscape plotted and pieced – fold, fallow, and plough;
And all trades, their gear and tackle and trim.

All things counter, original, spare, strange;
Whatever is fickle, freckled (who knows how?)
With swift, slow; sweet, sour; adazzle, dim;
He fathers-forth whose beauty is past change:
Praise him.

Fr John Bannister Tabb 1845-1909

Father Damien

O God, the cleanest offering
Of tainted earth below,
Unblushing to Thy feet we bring –
'A leper white as snow!'

Recognition

When Christ went up to Calvary,
His crown upon His head,
Each tree unto its fellow tree
In awful silence said:
'Behold the Gardener is He
Of Eden and Gethsemane!'

Is Thy Servant a Dog?

So *must* he be, who in the crowded street,
Where shameless Sin and flaunting Pleasure meet,
Amid the noisome footprints finds the sweet
Faint vestige of Thy feet.

The Annunciation

'*Fiat*!' – The flaming word[1]
Flashed, as the brooding bird
Uttered the doom far heard
Of death and night.

'*Fiat*!' – A cloistered womb –
A sealed, untainted tomb –
Wakes to the birth and bloom
Of life and light.

1. *Fiat*, Latin for 'let it be done'.

The Immaculate Conception

A dewdrop of the darkness born,
Wherein no shadow lies;
The blossom of a barren thorn,
Whereof no petal dies;
A rainbow beauty passion-free,
Wherewith was veiled Divinity.

Hilaire Belloc 1870-1953

Courtesy

Of Courtesy, it is much less
Than Courage of Heart or Holiness,
Yet in my walks it seems to me
That the Grace of God is in Courtesy.

On Monks I did in Storrington fall.
They took me straight into their Hall;
I saw three pictures on a wall,
And Courtesy was in them all.

The first the Annunciation;
The second the Visitation;

The third the Consolation,
Of God that was Our Lady's Son.

The first was of St Gabriel;
On wings a-flame from Heaven he fell;
And as he went upon one knee
He shone with heavenly Courtesy.

Our Lady out of Nazareth rode –
It was Her month of heavy load;
Yet was Her face both great and kind
For Courtesy was in Her Mind.

The third it was our Little Lord,
Whom all the Kings in arms adored;
He was so small you could not see
His large intent of Courtesy.

Our Lord, that was Our Lady's Son,
Go bless you, People, one by one;
My rhyme is written, my work is done.

The Prophet Lost in the Hills at Evening

Strong God which made the topmost stars
To circulate and keep their course,
Remember me; whom all the bars
Of sense and dreadful fate enforce.

Above me in your heights and tall,
Impassable the summits freeze,
Below the haunted waters call
Impassable beyond the trees.

I hunger and I have no bread.
My gourd is empty of the wine.
Surely the footsteps of the dead
Are shuffling softly close to mine!

It darkens. I have lost the ford.
There is a change on all things made.
The rocks have evil faces, Lord,
And I am awfully afraid.

Remember me! the voids of Hell
Expand enormous all around.
Strong friend of souls, Emmanuel,
Redeem me from accursed ground.

The long descent of wasted days,
To these at last have led me down;
Remember that I filled with praise
The meaningless and doubtful ways
That lead to an eternal town.

I challenged and I kept the Faith,
The bleeding path alone I trod;
It darkens. Stands about my wraith,
And harbour me – almighty God!

The Birds

When Jesus Christ was four years old,
The angels brought Him toys of gold,
Which no man ever had bought or sold.

And yet with these He would not play.
He made Him small fowl out of clay,
And blessed them till they flew away:
'Tu creasti Domine.'[1]

Jesus Christ, Thou child so wise,
Bless mine hands and fill mine eyes,
And bring my soul to Paradise.

1. *Tu creasti Domine* = You are our Creator, O Lord.

Lord Alfred Douglas 1870-1945

From *In Excelsis*

II

I follow honour, brokenly content,
Though the sick flesh repine, though darkness creep
Into the soul's unfathomable deep,
Where fear is bred: though from my spirit spent
Like poured-out water, the mind's weak consent
Be hardly wrung, while eyes too tired to weep
Dimly discern, as through a film of sleep,
Squalor that is my honour's ornament.

Without, the fire of earth-contemning stars
Burns in deep blueness, like an opal set
In jacinth borders underneath the moon.
The dappled shadow that my window bars
Cast on the wall is like a silver net.
My angel, in my heart, sings 'heaven soon'.

III

I have within me that which still defies
This generation's bloat intelligence,
Which is the advocate of my defence
Against the indictment of the world's assize.
Clutching with bleeding hands my hard-won prize,
Immeasurably bought by fierce expense
Of blood and sweat and spirit-harnessed sense,
I keep the steadfast gaze of tear-washed eyes.

And this discernment, not inherited,
But grimly conned in many cruel schools,
Unravels all illusion to my sight.
In vain, for me with wings, the snare is spread.
Folly imputed by the mouth of fools
Is wisdom's ensign to a child of light.

Mgr R.H. Benson 1871-1914

After a Retreat

What hast thou learnt today?
Hast thou sounded awful mysteries,
Hast pierced the veiled skies,
Climbed to the feet of God,
Trodden where saints have trod,
Fathomed the heights above? *Nay,*
This only have I learnt, that God is love.

What hast thou heard today?
Hast heard the angel-trumpets cry,
And rippling harps reply;
Heard from the throne of flame
Whence God incarnate came
Some thund'rous message roll? *Nay,*
This have I heard, His voice within my soul.

What hast thou felt today?
The pinions of the angel-guide
That standeth at thy side
In rapturous ardours beat,
Glowing, from head to feet,
In ecstasy divine? *Nay,*
This only have I felt, Christ's hand in mine.

The Priest's Lament

Lord, hast Thou set me here
Thy priest to be,
The burden of Thy yoke to bear,
To feel Thy cords about me set,
Wince at the lash, but never yet
Thy Face to see?

Lord, see what wounds on me
Thy burden makes!

Dost Thou despise my misery?
Ah, Master! Wilt Thou let me strain,
And fall and rise and fall again,
Till my heart breaks?

Lord, I am near to die,
So steep the hill,
So slow the wheels, so feeble I,
The halting place so far above.
Art Thou indeed a God of Love,
And tender still?

'Son, turn a moment, see
Is that blood thine?
Who is it shares thy yoke with thee,
Treads foot by foot with thee the road?
Whose shoulder bears the heavier load,
Is it not Mine?'

The Teresian Contemplative

She moves in tumult; round her lies
The silence of the world of grace;
The twilight of our mysteries
Shines like high noonday on her face;
Our piteous guesses, dim with fears,
She touches, handles, sees, and hears.

In her all longings mix and meet;
Dumb souls through her are eloquent;
She feels the world beneath her feet
Thrill in a passionate intent;
Through her our tides of feeling roll
And find their God within her soul.

Her faith the awful Face of God
Brightens and blinds with utter light;
Her footsteps fall where late He trod;

She sinks in roaring voids of night;
Cries to her Lord in black despair,
And knows, yet knows not, He is there.

A willing sacrifice she takes
The burden of our fall within;
Holy she stands; while on her breaks
The lightning of the wrath of sin;
She drinks her Saviour's cup of pain,
And, one with Jesus, thirsts again.

Wedding Hymn

Father, within thy House today
We wait Thy kindly love to see;
Since Thou hast said in truth that they
Who dwell in love are one with Thee,
Bless those who for Thy blessing wait,
Their love accept and consecrate.

Dear Lord of love, whose Heart of Fire,
So full of pity for our sin,
Was once in that Divine Desire
Broken, Thy Bride to woo and win:
Look down and bless them from above
And keep their hearts alight with love.

Blest Spirit, who with life and light
Didst quicken chaos to Thy praise,
Whose energy, in sin's despite,
Still lifts our nature up to grace;
Bless those who here in troth consent.
Creator, crown Thy Sacrament.

Great One in Three, of Whom are named
All families in earth and heaven,
Hear us, who have Thy promise claimed,
And let a wealth of grace be given;

Grant them in life and death to be
Each knit to each, and both to Thee.

G.K. Chesterton 1874-1936

The Donkey

When fishes flew and forests walked
And figs grew upon thorn,
Some moment when the moon was blood
Then surely I was born.

With monstrous head and sickening cry
And ears like errant wings,
The devil's walking parody
On all four-footed things.

The tattered outlaw of the earth,
Of ancient crooked will;
Starve, scourge, deride me: I am dumb,
I keep my secret still.

Fools! For I also had my hour;
One far fierce hour and sweet:
There was a shout about my ears,
And palms before my feet.

The Convert[1]

After one moment when I bowed my head
And the whole world turned over and came upright,
And I came out where the old road shone white,
I walked the ways and heard what all men said,
Forests of tongues, like autumn leaves unshed,
Being not unlovable but strange and light;
Old riddles and new creeds, not in despite
But softly, as men smile about the dead.

The sages have a hundred maps to give
That trace their crawling cosmos like a tree,
They rattle reason out through many a sieve
That stores the sand and lets the gold go free:
And all these things are less than dust to me
Because my name is Lazarus and I live.

1. Poem written on Chesterton's reception into the Catholic Church on
30 July 1922.

Thomas MacDonagh 1878-1916

To My Newborn Son – St Cecilia's Day 1912

Now, my son, is life for you,
And I wish you joy of it, –
Joy of power in all you do,
Deeper passion, better wit
Than I had who had enough,
Quicker life and length thereof,
More of every gift but love.

Love I have beyond all men,
Love that now you share with me –
What have I to wish you then
But that you be good and free,
And that God to you may give
Grace in stronger days to live?

For I wish you more than I
Ever knew of glorious deed,
Though no rapture passed me by
That an eager heart could heed,
Though I followed heights and sought
Things the sequel never brought:

Wild and perilous holy things
Flaming with a martyr's blood,
And the joy that laughs and sings

Where a foe must be withstood,
Joy of headlong happy chance
Leading on the battle dance.

But I found no enemy,
No man in a world of wrong,
That Christ's word of Charity
Did not render clean and strong –
Who was I to judge my kind,
Blindest groper of the blind?

God to you may give the sight
And the clear undoubting strength
Wars to knit for single right,
Freedom's war to knit at length,
And to win, through wrath and strife,
To the sequel of my life,

But for you, so small and young,
Born on St Cecilia's Day,
I in more harmonious song
Now for nearer joys should pray –

Simple joys: the natural growth
Of your childhood and your youth.
Courage, innocence, and truth:

These for you, so small and young,
In your hand and heart and tongue.

Padraic Colum 1881-1972

Christ the Comrade

Christ, by Thine own darkened hour
Live within my heart and brain!
Let my hands not slip the rein.

Ah, how long ago it is
Since a comrade rode with me!
Now a moment let me see.

Thyself, lonely in the dark,
Perfect, without wound or mark!

A Cradle Song

O men from the fields,
Come gently within.
Tread softly, softly,
O men coming in!

Mavourneen is going[1]
From me and from you,
Where Mary will fold him
With mantle of blue!

From reek of the smoke
And cold of the floor
And the peering of things
Across the half-door.

O men of the fields,
Soft, softly come thro'.
Mary puts round him
Her mantle of blue.

1. Mavourneen = my darling.

Joyce Kilmer 1886-1918

Prayer of a Soldier in France

My shoulders ache beneath the pack
(Lie easier, Cross, upon His back).

I march with feet that burn and smart
(Tread, Holy Feet, upon my heart).

Men shout at me who may not speak
(They scourged Thy back and smote Thy cheek).

I may not lift a hand to clear
My eyes of salty drops that sear.

(Then shall my fickle soul forget
Thy Agony of Bloody Sweat?)

My rifle hand is stiff and numb
(From Thy pierced palm red rivers come)

Lord, Thou didst suffer more for me
Than all the hosts of land and sea.

So, let me render back again
This millionth of Thy gift. Amen.

The Singing Girl

There was a little maiden
In blue and silver dressed,
She sang to God in Heaven
And God within her breast.

It flooded me with pleasure,
It pierced me like a sword,
When this young maiden sang: 'my soul
Doth magnify the Lord.'

The stars sing all together
And hear the angels sing
But they said they had never heard
So beautiful a thing.

St Mary and St Joseph,
And St Elizabeth,
Pray for us poets now
And at the hour of our death.

Joseph Mary Plunkett 1887-1916

I See His Blood upon the Rose

I see His blood upon the rose
And in the stars the glory of His eyes,
His body gleams amid eternal snows,
His tears fall from the skies.

I see His face in every flower;
The thunder and the singing of the birds
Are but His voice – and carven by His power
Rocks are His written words.

All pathways by His feet are worn,
His strong heart stirs the ever-beating sea,
His crown of thorns is twined with every thorn,
His cross is every tree.

The Stars Sang in God's Garden

The stars sang in God's garden;
The stars are the birds of God;
The night-time is God's harvest,
Its fruits are the words of God.

God ploughed His fields at morning,
God sowed His seed at noon,
God reaped and gathered in His corn
With the rising of the moon.

The sun rose up at midnight,
The sun rose red as blood,
It showed the Reaper, the dead Christ,
Upon His cross of wood.

For many live that one may die,
And one must die that many live –
The stars are silent in the sky
Lest my poor songs be fugitive.

Theodore Maynard 1890-1956

A Song of Colours

Gold for the crown of Mary,
Blue for the sea and sky,
Green for the woods and the meadows
Where small white daisies lie,
And red for the colour of Christ's blood
When He came to the cross to die.

These things the high God gave us
And left in the world He made –
Gold for the hilt's enrichment,
And blue for the sword's good blade,
And red for the roses a youth may set
On the white brows of a maid.

Green for the cool, sweet gardens
Which stretch about the house,
And the delicate new frondage
The winds of spring arouse,
And red for the wine which a man may drink
With his fellows in carouse.

Blue and green for the comfort
Of tired hearts and eyes,
And red for that sudden hour which comes
With danger and great surprise,
And white for the honour of God's throne
When the dead shall all arise.

Gold for the cope and chalice,
For kingly pomp and pride,
And red for the feathers men wear in their caps
When they win a war or a bride,
And red for the robe which they dressed God in,
On the bitter day He died.

Cecidit, Cecidit Babylon Magna! (Babylon the Great has Passed Away)

The aimless business of your feet,
Your swinging wheels and piston rods,
The smoke of every sullen street
Have passed away with all your gods.

For in a meadow far from these
A hodman treads across the loam,
Bearing his solid sanctities
To that strange altar called his home.

I watch the tall, sagacious trees
Turn as the monks do, every one;
The saplings, ardent novices,
Turning with them towards the sun,

That Monstrance held in God's strong hands,
Burnished in amber and in red;
God, His own Priest, in blessing stands;
The earth, adoring, bows her head.

The idols of your market place,
Your high debates, where are they now?
Your lawyers' clamour fades apace –
A bird is singing on the bough!

Three fragile, sacramental things
Endure, though all your pomps shall pass –
A butterfly's immortal wings,
A daisy, and a blade of grass.

Wilfred Rowland Childe 1890-1952

Hoc Est Corpus Meum (This Is My Body)

They are gone hunting for Thy soul, O Lord,
Deep-diving down into time's endless wells:

Profounder than all sounds of chanting and bells,
They have let slip their learning's lengthy cord.

One man will put Thee with the Greeks to school,
And many books they have written mighty and wise,
And one a prophet makes Thee with pale eyes,
And one a madman or a dreaming fool.

Yet still at certain times the steps are trod,
Yet still at certain times the words are said;
Thou dost present Thyself to be our bread,
And we are nourished with the Body of God.

Latens Deitas (Hidden Godhead)

Thee I adore, O hidden Saviour, Thee,
Dwelling within the sacramental veils,
Whose presence in my heart's shrine never fails,
Abiding in most patient mystery.
Behind the beauteous garments of Thy world
I worship Thee, symbolled by star-clean flowers,
Or by remote blue air of hesperal hours,
With thin white clouds and plaintive moon-beams pearled.
The loveliness of Thy creation shows Thee,
Whose Precious Blood in streams that never tire
Whelms all that lives in Eucharistic bliss:
The faithful heart of Thy poor servant knows Thee,
When Thy sweet transubstantiating Kiss
Burns up all life in spiritual fire.

Patrick Kirby 1891-1950

Sequel to Finality

They drove the hammered nails into His hands,
His hands that shaped the hot sun overhead;
Then all prepared to return to their own lands,
Glad in the knowledge God at last was dead.

'Now Babel can be built, and none deny!
In its cool gardens shall we take our ease;
Nor need we fear the everseeing eye,
Our gods shall be whatever gods we please.

Ishtar shall guard us, mother of all men,
And Bel rejoice us when the winds blow spiced
From Indus. Wine and song shall glad us then,
We never loved this wistful, pallid Christ!'

So each rode homeward. And by each one's side
Unseen One rode, Who had been crucified.

Consecration

Silence – and a muted bell rings;
Old words are spoken in an ancient tongue;
And music ceases; before these Holy things
Be song unsung.

Within this Holy place none trod
Until the High Priest opened wide the door;
Now God and man are mingled in one God!
Kneel and adore!

Across the wine-cup trembling hands
Move cruciform – 'these things – remembering Me';
Lifting a deathless Christ, the Cross stands
At Calvary!

David Jones 1895-1974

A, a, a, Domine Deus

I said, Ah! what shall I write?
I enquired up and down.
(He's tricked me before with his manifold lurking-places.)
I looked for His symbol at the door.
I have looked for a long while at the textures and contours.
I have run a hand over the trivial intersections.

270

I have journeyed among the dead forms –
causation projects from pillar to pylon.
I have tired the eyes of the mind regarding the colours
    and lights.
I have felt for His Wounds in nozzles and containers.
I have wondered for the automatic devices.
I have tested the inane patterns without prejudice.
I have been on my guard not to condemn the unfamiliar.
For it is easy to miss Him at the turn of a civilisation.

I have watched the wheels go round in case I might see the
living creatures like the appearance of lamps, in case I might
see the Living God projected from the Machine. I have said
to the perfected steel, be my sister and for the glassy towers
I thought I felt some beginnings of His creature, but *A, a, a,
Domine Deus,* my hands found the glazed work unrefined
and the terrible crystal a stage-paste … *Eia, Domine Deus.*

Fr Leo Ward 1896-1942

Four Friends

Full life, sweet rest, great love that cannot cease –
Surely Bach saw the beatific host!
As the deep waters of the Holy Ghost
On young Mozart rained purity and ease –
'Twas a full heart, God-centred and at peace;
While, from that awful gloom where souls are lost,
Or raised to the height of hope, confessed and crossed
The vision of Beethoven sought release,

Taking each beam of grace that pierced his world
To light the fearsome steps from hell to Heaven
And paint the hard-won victory over death! …
And now upon life's battle Franck has hurled
The mystery of Christ: yea, death is riven,
And nature one with God, at Nazareth!

The Lost Communion (In Memory of My Father Leo Ward)

There is a time wherein eternity
Takes rest upon the world; King Charity
Bowed to our fallen state, the God of Grace
Made visible upon a human face;
When the deep Harmony, the eternal Word,
The unfallen wisdom, only love has heard,
Touches the troubled body, bruised and hard
With the long fight, yet now set heavenward,
When the deep argument of souls must cease,
Dying, to meet the victory of peace!

Sr Maris Stella 1899-

It is the Reed

I did not cut myself this hollow reed,
I did not seek it in the shallows growing.
In all my life I paid but little heed
To burnished reeds in the bright shallows blowing.
And this that now is thrust into my hand
Mysteriously cut and tuned for singing
Was gathered in a strange and distant land
And has immortal airs about it clinging.
An unseen piper tuned its ghostly note.
O who would dare to touch it – who would dare?
From out the fearful hollow of its throat
Such music pours as I am unaware
How to devise. I did not think these things.
It is the reed, it is the reed that sings.

I Who Had Been Afraid

I who had been afraid of the dark at night
As a child here in this room, even when I lay
Safe by my mother's bed, now without fright
Watched here alone until the break of day

My mother lying in the last sleep of all.
Never would she wake into the night again.
Here was the beautiful end. No child would call,
No grief disturb, no terrible, torturing pain
Constrain her from the quiet. Here was at last
Catharsis – all pity and terror spent.
Sorrow, splendour, living, dying – past.
All things fulfilled and nothing to lament.
I who had been afraid of the darkness, here
Alone with the beloved dead found nothing to fear.

Love is not Solace

Love is not solace else it is not love
That binds me here against the body's cry
Within such bonds as I am mistress of
Yet will not ever loose until I die.
Love is not warmth and brightness since I know
Darkness and cold as well as day and night.
Forewarned of mutability I go
With frugal comfort through the shifting light.
Love is not love that for love will not lack
The bread of sweetness and the wine of tears,
Nor dare to relish hunger and the rack,
Nor weigh it overmuch nor count the years,
But will endure through bounty and through dearth,
A deep-heard river in the heart's deep earth.

The Voice

I am afraid of silence. I am afraid
Of my own soul. I am afraid of hearing
A voice – one voice above all voices – made
Clear in the silence. I shall grow old fearing
This silence that goes with me wherever I go.
I cannot keep it in or bar it out.
Always within, around, above, below,
It beats upon me. I am hedged about

Most utterly. Surrounded. Yet I raise
Even now a futile barrier of sound
Against the voice in silence I dispraise,
Against the voice I dread that hems me round;
To which, did I but listen, I should be
Afraid of nothing. Nothing could frighten me.

Caryll Houselander 1901-1954

Philip Speaks

When we returned and told Him all we had done,
I for one was emptied out like a husk
that has scattered its seed upon hard ground.

We had not had time even to eat;
always the open hand,
always the blind eyes,
always the deaf ears,
always the wound to be healed.

My thoughts were like wild birds
beating the bars of the cage
for empty skies.

Even now the smell of the people
clung to my hair and clothes,
a rotten sweetness of oil and musk
that smells like death, it hung in my hair.

Their voices went on and on in my head,
monotonous waves wearing my mind away;
rock is worn by the waves to sand.
I wanted to shut my mind, that my thoughts might close
on my own peace, I wanted to close
the peace of my love in my heart
like dew in a dark rose.

He told us to rest.

We went in a small ship,
the wind and water moving in her,
She lived in their sweetness of life, a bride.
Her sail a white wing, unmoving, moved with the tide.
She lay to the wind, and we gave our hearts with a sigh
to the breath of the spirit of love.

But when we came to the shore
the people were there;
they had found us out.
Always the open hand,
always the blind eyes,
always the deaf ears,
always the wounds to be healed!
They were there,
swarming there, everywhere,
insects there in the sun
when someone has lifted a stone.
I knew they would drain Him
and wring Him out – wring Him out
to the last drop of the fountain water of Life.

I was sick of it all
with a dry husk for a heart.
But He saw the flocks wanting shepherd and fold,
pity in Him rose in a clear spring
for the world's thirst, and love was a pastureland.

So it went on all day.
Always the open hand,
always the dull mind,
always the slow heart
always the nameless fears, and self-pity, self-pity and tears;

Until the sun went up in the blaze of the day's heat
and with red wine burning through thin gold
it was lowered slowly on to the altar stone
of the darkening world, where the sheep were in fold.

We thought 'Now it is night, He will send them away,
The hour is late,' we said, 'this is a desert place,
send them away, Lord, to buy food and be fed!'
But He 'You give them to eat!'

The grass in that place shone exceedingly green,
I remember, because when the brain is dust,
the cool greenness of grass is absurdly sweet.
'There is a lad here,' said Andrew,
'With two little fish and five loaves of bread,
but what are these, if this crowd must be fed?'
'Bid them sit down on the grass and give them to eat'
the Lord said.
The lad was one of the crowd, he went as he came.
As long as the world lasts, the world will remember him,
but no one will know his name!

They sat down on the grass.
My heart contracted, my mind was withered up,
but Christ poured out His tenderness,
like wine poured out into a lifted cup.

Always the open hands,
always the blind eyes,
always the mouth to be fed,
and I for one was emptied out like a husk
that has scattered its seed upon hard ground.
But He saw the flocks wanting shepherd and fold;
Pity in Him rose in a clear spring
for the world's thirst, and love was a pastureland.

The Lord blessed the bread.
He put it into our hands
and it multiplied,
not in *His* hands but in *mine!*

Even now, remembering this,
my thoughts shut like a folding wing,

my mind is a blank sheet of light
in the mystery of the thing.

I gave and my hands were full, again and again;
Pity in Him fell on my dry dust,
it was summer rain,
and the husk of my heart expanded and filled again,
and was large with grain.

For me, the miracle was this,
that a clear stream of the Lord's love
(not mine)
flowed out of my soul,
a shining wave, over my fellow men.

These things I have told you happened a long while since.
Our cherished Lord is dead, He was crucified.
Now, as then, we go about in the crowd telling His love,
and how He rose from the dead, and risen in us
He lives in the least of men.
But I think nobody understands,
until I touch their wounds and they know
the healing of *His* hands.

On the night of the Pasch, before He died,
He blessed the bread and put it into my hands,
to increase and be multiplied to the end of time.

Now if I turned my face away from the market place,
I should be haunted,
hearing the rustle of wheat in the darkness,
striving, pushing up to the light.
I should hear His words falling like slow tears
in the Supper room, –
when He prayed that we all be one,
even as they are one, the Father and Son, –
falling like slow tears over the sown fields,

and I should see the world
like a young field of wheat
growing up for the grain
watered by Christ's tears.

Always the open hands,
always the blind eyes,
always the slow mind,
always the deaf ears,
and always Christ, Our Lord,
crowned with the flowering thorn
and ringed with spears.

I know, – now that I never see
the print of His feet in the dust
where the Son of Man trod, –
that in every man for ever
I meet the Son of God.

Mediocracy

All the young men
and all the young women,
Hope for security,
A mild prosperity.
Respectability,
And a dull old age.

They want the Sunday smell.
Beef in a dead Street.
Six days to be bored,
And one to overeat.

Poor little birds in a cage!
Sitting behind the bars
It isn't life,
It's the living wage,
And the night without the stars.

God Abides in Man

God abides in men.
There are some men who are simple,
they are fields of corn.
We see the soil and the stubble,
more than the green spears
and the yellow stalks.
Such men have minds
like wide grey skies,
they have the grandeur that
The fool calls emptiness.

God is clothed in homespun in such lives.
He goes with them to the field and the barn,
He comes home, when the birds,
in dark orderly flocks
cross the empty twilights of time.

God abides in men.
Some men are not simple,
they live in cities
among the teeming buildings,
wrestling with forces
as strong as the sun and the rain.
Often they must forgo dream upon dream.
The glare of the electric light
blinds their eyes to the stars.
On some nights,
the stir of life, and the lights
is a soft fire, like wine in their blood.

Christ walks in the wilderness
in such lives.
Wrestling with Lucifer,
the fallen angel of light,
who shows Him the cities of the world,
and with brilliant and illimitable audacity,

offers to Christianity
lordship of the cities
on the world's terms.

God abides in men.
There are some men,
on whom the sins of the world are laid.
They are conscripted,
stripped, measured and weighed,
taken away from home,
and sent to the flood,
the fire, the darkness,
the loneliness of death.

In such men
Christ is stripped of His garments,
the reed is put in His hand,
the soldier's cloak on His shoulders,
the Cross on His back.
In them He is crucified.
From the lives,
and the deaths
of those men,
cities rise from the dead.

God abides in men,
because Christ has put on
the nature of man, like a garment,
and worn it to His own shape.

He has put on everyone's life.
He has fitted Himself to the little child's dress
to the shepherd's coat of sheepskin,
to the workman's coat,
to the King's red robes,
to the snowy loveliness of the wedding garment,
and to the drab
of the sad, simple battle dress.

Christ has put on Man's nature,
and given him back his humanness,
worn to the shape
of limitless love,
and warm from the touch
of His life.

He has given man his crown,
the thorn that is jewelled
with drops of His blood.
He has given him
the seamless garment
of his truth.
He has bound him
in the swaddling bands
of his humility.
He has fastened his hands
to the tree of life.
He has latched his feet
in crimson sandals,
that they move not
from the path of love.

God abides in man.

Low Mass on Sunday (extract)

The church is noisy with shuffle of children's feet,
and somebody's endless cough.
The heads of the boys in rows
are knobs of unpolished wood,
mahogany, teak, and pine.
Only the little Belgian,
son of the delicatessen,
has an ebony polished knob.

A tiny girl has come in late,
she is wearing a grown-up hat

and a jersey down to her knees.
The benches are full, but still,
there is room for the little girl,
as an old, old mumbling man,
who is small like a withered berry,
shrinks, smaller still, for her sake.

A thin young mother is smiling,
while fidgeting on her lap,
her grave round baby grabs
and puts on his father's hat.
He is staring with shadowless eyes,
immense in solemnity,
but the rigid father, dismayed
gives him a rosary
for plaything, in case he cries.
Gives him a string of beads,
because they are bright and small
to fit the size of his hand,
as God the Father of all,
to us the witless and weak,
gives gently the mysteries
of the life of His only Son,
to hush the possible cries
of spirits too small to hold
the simplicity of His love.

We are the common bread,
we are flesh and blood,
we are salt.
It is strange to think that the saints,
with their delicate smile of peace
carved in stone, and the flowers
withering at their feet,
were also the common bread,
and were flesh and blood
and were salt.

Not with the crystal peace,
held up to receive the light
we come, but tangled with care.
Deep in the earth our roots,
locked in the earth we know.
We are knit by a single thread,
a rhythm of fear; we are one
at least in this. Like the many
separate leaves on a bough
turned by a gust of wind
to a single fluttering wave.

Roy Campbell 1901-1957

The Mocking Bird

Like an old Cobra broken with a stick,
As in the ward with other crocks I lay
(Flies on the roof their sole arithmetic
Which they must count to pass the time of day) –
Born of my wound, or out of Bosch remembered,
Or by my own delirium designed,
A strange blue bird, it seemed I knew the kind
And the fierce look with which his eyes were embered,
For they had been spectators of the Fall-
Perched on my foot, I knew his ringing call,
And 'Shoo!' I cried, 'you phantom, fade away!
For here are canyons forested with sleep,
The woods are silent, and the shades are deep,
While you intrude the colours of the day.
I flinch before your lit triumphal pinion,
Your bloodshot gaze, the memory of strife,
Your cry, the laughing mockery of Life,
So raucous here, where sleep should have dominion!'
But as he would have flown I rose to follow,
A will was born where all things else were hollow,
And through those caverns of ancestral cedar

Where all but downward streams had lost their way
His voice of mocking laughter was my leader –
The blue hallucination of a jay!

Mass at Dawn

I dropped my sail and dried my dripping seines
Where the white quay is chequered by cool planes
In whose great branches, always out of sight,
The nightingales are singing day and night.
Though all was grey beneath the moon's grey beam,
My boat in her new paint shone like a bride,
And silver in my baskets shone the bream:
My arms were tired and I was heavy-eyed,
But when with food and drink, at morning-light,
The children met me at the water-side,
Never was wine so red or bread so white.

Christ in the Hospital (at Padre Evaristo, Carmelita Descalzo, Toledo)

Ixions of the slow wheel of the day
They had come down at last, but not to stay,
And at the fall of night, with even sway,
Were slowly wheeling up the other way.

And he who felt the finest in the Ward
Was scarcely better than a broken stick;
His spine ran through him like a rusty sword
Rasping its meagre scabbard to the quick.

Through the dim pane he saw the stars take flight
Like pigeons scattered by the crash and groan
Of the great world, with pendulum of stone
Dingdonging in the steeple of the Night.

He heard, far off, the people stream their course
Whipped by their pleasures into frantic tops –

As the grey multitude (when twilight drops)
Goes out to trade its boredom for remorse.

The Moon, a soldier with a bleeding eye,
Returning to the war, beheld these things.
And long grey tom-cats crept across the sky
Between the chimneys where the wireless sings.

Never seemed anything so steep or tall
(Sierra, iceberg, or the tower of noon),
As what he saw when turning from the moon –
The bloody Christ that hung upon the wall!

Great Albatross, of every storm the Birth!-
His bleeding pinions bracketed a Night
Too small for His embrace; and from his height,
As from an Eagle's, cowered the plaintive Earth!

Translations from St John of the Cross

V

About the Soul Which Suffers With Impatience to See God
I live without inhabiting
Myself – in such a wise that I
Am dying that I do not die.

Within myself I do not dwell
Since without God I cannot live.
Reft of myself, and God as well,
What serves this life (I cannot tell)
Except a thousand deaths to give?
Since waiting here for life I lie
And die because I do not die.

This life I live in vital strength
Is loss of life unless I win You:
And thus to die I shall continue
Until in You I live at length.

Listen (my God!) my life is in You.
This life I do not want, for I
Am dying that I do not die.

Thus in your absence and your lack
How can I in myself abide
Nor suffer here a death more black
Than ever was by mortal died.
For pity of myself I've cried
Because in such a plight I lie
Dying because I do not die.

The fish that from the stream is lost
Derives some sort of consolation
That in his death he pays the cost
At least of death's annihilation.
To this dread life with which I'm crossed
What fell death can compare, since I,
The more I live, the more must die.

When thinking to relieve my pain
I in the sacraments behold You
It brings me greater grief again
That to myself I cannot fold You.
And that I cannot see You plain
Augments my sorrow, so that I
Am dying that I do not die.

If in the hope I should delight,
Oh Lord, of seeing You appear,
The thought that I might lose Your sight
Doubles my sorrow and my fear.
Living as I do in such fright,
And yearning as I yearn, poor I
Must die because I do not die.

Oh rescue me from such a death
My God, and give me life, not fear;

Nor keep me bound and struggling here
Within the bonds of living breath.
Look how I long to see You near,
And how in such a plight I lie
Dying because I do not die!

I shall lament my death betimes,
And mourn my life, that it must be
Kept prisoner by sins and crimes
So long before I am set free:
Ah God, my God, when shall it be?
When I may say (and tell no lie)
I live because I've ceased to die?

XX

With a Divine Intention, by the Same Author
For all the beauty life has got
I'll never throw myself away
Save for one thing I know not what
Which lucky chance may bring my way.

The savour of all finite joy
In the long run amounts to this –
To tire the appetite of bliss
And the fine palate to destroy.
So for life's sweetness, all the lot,
I'll never throw myself away
But for a thing, I know not what,
Which lucky chance may bring my way.

The generous heart upon its quest
Will never falter, nor go slow,
But pushes on, and scorns to rest,
Wherever it's most hard to go.
It runs ahead and wearies not
But upward hurls its fierce advance

For it enjoys I know not what
That is achieved by lucky chance.

He that is growing to full growth
In the desire of God profound,
Will find his tastes so changed around
That of mere pleasures he is loth,
Like one who, with the fever hot,
At food will only look askance
But craves for that, he knows not what,
Which may be brought by lucky chance.

Do not amaze yourself at this
That pleasure is of earthly things
That cause from which most evil springs
And most the enemy of bliss.
And so all creatures, earth-begot
Begin from it to turn their glance
And seek a thing, I know not what,
Which may be won by lucky chance.

For once the will has felt the hand
Of the Divine upon it set,
It never ceases to demand,
Divinity must pay the debt.
But since its loveliness to scan
Only true faith may steal a glance,
It finds it out as best it can
By risking on a lucky chance.

With love of One so high elated,
Tell me, if you would find great harm
If the servants He created
Did not rival Him in charm?
Alone, without face, form, or features,
Foothold, or prop, you would advance
To love that thing, beyond all creatures,
Which may be won by happy chance.

Think not that the interior sprite
Which is of vastly greater worth,
Can find among the joys of earth
Much for amusement or delight.
This world no beauty can advance
Which is, or ever was begot,
To vie with that, I know not what,
Which may be won by lucky chance.

The man who strains for wealth and rank
Employs more care, and wastes more health
For riches that elude his stealth
Than those he's hoarded in the bank;
But I my fortune to advance
The lowlier stoop my lowly lot
Over some thing, I know not what,
Which may be found by lucky chance.

For that which by the sense down here
Is comprehended as our good,
And all that can be understood
Although it soars sublime and sheer;
For all that beauty can enhance –
I'll never lose my happy lot:
Only for that, I know not what,
Which can be won by lucky chance.

XXI

Concerning the Divine Word
With the divinest word, the Virgin
Made pregnant, down the road
Comes walking, if you'll grant her
A room in your abode.

XXII

Summary of Perfection
Ignoring the created and inferior;
Remember above all things the Creator;
Attention to the life that is interior;
For the Beloved love that's always greater.

Fr John W. Lynch 1904-

The Crucifixion

He is alive with pain: His body lifts
And turns and quivers as the lightning streaks
Again, and iron thunder cracks and breaks
And shatters in the dark beneath His blood;
Until the tremors in His flesh are stopped,
And breathing, He discovers He is vised.
His body forms a frame to hold a frame;
He is a Man made one with blunted beams!...
Their voices rise to Him from distant pits.
They are like echoes of an ended world
He once had known where men with hands and feet
Could move among contentions and be brave
With gesture. He could hear them, feel their stride
And strut along the ground, receive their scorn,
Their laughter, know that they were tall and bold
And beckoning to Him that He come down,
Come down and be a Man again in whole,
Unfastened body that will need a robe
And pathway to the pardons of the world.

'Father, forgive them, for they know not what they do.'

The blood swelled sickly in His mouth, and breath
Was ended, and His heart was all he heard.
Somewhere, as a bird might sing to Him,
Above Him, level to His hair, so near

He need not search, nor move, nor seek for space
Of quiet in the sounding of His blood,
He hears a voice that begs last royal gift
Of brief remembering. He cannot see,
And wrenching now athwart the rigid wood,
His head uplifted, pulling at the nails,
He cannot reach least moment of relief
That He may bring to eyes that seek His own.
They are two faces in the sun, so fixed
Against the posts they must stare outward only,
Separate, and must declare their loves
In quick companionship of lonely words.

'This day thou shalt be with me in Paradise.'

The light is bronze against Him in a sheet
Of stilled, unblinking time that does not move,
Nor yield, nor cease until a shimmering
Like golden curtains comes, and looking down,
He finds that time has folded to a long,
Bright, gleaming coronal, and she is there.
He does not look away, He watches her,
And the light that was a crown about her, breaks,
Increases, brightens, and becomes a path
Where she is mounting, mounting up to Him,
Not for comfort, not for any kiss
Of soothing, not to lessen Him nor ask
His hands refuse these nails for Infancy:
Not to soften, not unloose the years!
He seeks her here and in her heart He finds
Too deep a silence for the need of tears,
For new Announcement bleeds in her, so old
It is Gethsemani, and Nazareth,
Fused and sealed within a single will
That still is crying: *'This be done to me.'*

'Woman, behold thy Son.'

The dark was like a thin, descending shroud
Of cold that closed around the world and left
Him shivering beneath an ashen sun.
The wind was chill upon Him, stirred His hair
In faint and lonely movement, and the dust
That lay along the barren rocks had raised
And sifted softly when the wind had gone.
He was alone: and in His hands the nails
Were cinders of a fire once had flamed
And reddened in His blood, but now had dulled
To crusting of a spread, accustomed pain,
Without a plan. He had wearied Of His crown;
His head that had been bowed upon His breast
Tossed upward in a search for any friend,
To find around Him blackness and the deep,
Unstarred abysses where creation's Word
Has hung no light or mercy to the blank
Rejections of a worse than primal dark.
The wind that knifed across His shivered soul
Came cutting from the frozen lids of Hell…

'My God, my God, why hast Thou forsaken me?'

Thereafter time on Him became a slow,
Eventless draining and His body sagged
And ebbed and whitened in the drip of long,
Increasing silences that breathed and soaked
And mingled on His limbs until the flow
Pulled down from Him all semblance to a Man,
To make Him but a Wound that hung from nails.

He does not move nor murmur to the dark,
And now is gone beyond His search or hope
For friends who might, in grieving, come to Him;
His eyes lie closed, but when His hand had strained

Against the stake, and helpless, tried to brush
The dried and stiffened cavern of His mouth,
He whispered, and they heard His human need.

'I thirst.'

A sponge upon a reed was thrust to Him,
And He who gave good wine had tasted sharp,
Astringent vinegars that were the last
Of favours that the earth could give to Him.
He wakened: He was tall again and taut
Against the throning of His cross; His head
Was crowned, and on Him majesty returned.
He drank the air and as a Man who sees
Far kingdoms over continents beyond
The sun, He traces with His eyes the dim
Receding circles of the world. He feels
The freedom of His hands, the swing, the lope
And striding of His feet; He feels His heart
Within Him beating to the endless stroke
Of Infinite, and swelling to subdue
The vast dimensions of forgotten time.
He stands, He towers, He is Adam come
Again to the ancient garden: He is man
And woman, He is Paul and Magdalen
The martyrs, housewives, sinners, and the saints.

And then His love is falling on the hills,
The roads, the little sea that had been dear.
He touches to the mountains where He spoke
His prayer, and He remembers Bread. His hands
Enclose again the smiling of a child.
They test the tumult of the fish in nets.
He hears the echoed word He said to John
And Martha: Peter keeps command against
The years. The cot and table that He knew
At Nazareth are not afar from Him.

And He remembers Joseph and the straw:

Then breath is great within Him. He is tall
And upward from His cross His voice ascends
To break confining spaces of the stars
And thrust His triumph past the end of stars.

'It is finished!'

His head is sinking: peace is on His brow.

'Father, into Thy hands I commend my spirit.'

This sterile wood He carried to the hill
Has burgeoned with His meaning, and the Tree
Of good and evil, standing in all storm
And contradiction, waits the endless Spring.

Patrick Kavanagh 1905-1967

Street Corner Christ

I saw Christ today
At a street corner stand,
In the rags of a beggar he stood
He held ballads in his hand.

He was crying out: 'Two for a penny
Will anyone buy
The finest ballads ever made
From the stuff of joy?'

But the blind and deaf went past
Knowing only there
An uncouth ballad seller
With tail-matted hair.

And I whom men call fool
His ballads bought,
Found Him whom the pieties
Have vainly sought.

Beyond the Headlines

Then I saw the wild geese flying
In fair formation to their bases in Inchicore
And I knew that these wings would outwear the wings
   of war
And a man's simple thoughts outlive the day's loud lying.
'Don't fear, don't fear', I said to my soul.
'The Bedlam of Time is an empty bucket rattled,
'Tis you who will say in the end who best battles.
Only they who fly home to God have flown at all.'

Fr Alfred Barrett SJ 1906-

Chant of Departure – A Missionary's Prayer

Woman who walked home on the arm of John
Another way from that your Son had gone,
Woman who walked
And talked,
Unwavering, of what must yet be done –
Woman, behold your son!

Behold
Him who in boyhood haunts will not grow old;
Who goes predestined to an alien grave
In clay or sand or wave –
Yet sails enamoured of one hope: to see,
As John, from his dawn-lit boat on Galilee,
Christ in the haze-dim faces on the shore
At Shantung or the coast of Travancore.
Woman who walked home on the arm of John,

When on
Some night of tears I hear the palm trees toss,
Stand by my side beneath the Southern Cross.

Meriol Trevor 1919-2000

The Tower of Babel and the Pentecostal Fire

Once in a tower language was broken,
By the cyclone of darkness the tower was shaken:
This tower is the figure of man
Raising his fort against the divine sun.

He set up his will, brick by brick:
At every course the steep tower shook,
In all its mansions quarrels grew sharper
Yet without plans up went the skyscraper.

The fall of this tower was caused by fission
And the dust rose like a flower of damnation,
From the split minds spat the split tongues
And the broken fountains of all our songs.

In the city of Jerusalem was a room
Where a woman and twelve sad men came,
They began to pray and the house to shiver
In the first gust of the divine lover.

The descent was fire: like the flashing trickle
Of forked lightning it fell on that circle
And their tongues leapt with spiritual flame:
In every heart the Word struck home.

The tower of this world is a tree of dust
And its tongues like snakes rattle in the waste;
But in the middle the Ghost is hidden
And the Body will rise, whole and sudden.

John Bradburne 1921-1979

Spring is in the Air

The thought of God is written in the air,
 Weather and wind express Him with His Word,
Behold the hills so high above low care
 And hark to Yahweh's Voice in larksong heard;
The Thought of God is God the Father good;
 The Word of God expresses what God thinks,
The Voice of God wings vibrant in the wood
 Singing, or in our hearts with silence links;
These Three are Love Begetting Love Begotten
 And Love Proceeding as the Voice of both;
Love is Our God and King and nothing loth
 To sink into the silence, unforgotten:
  Switch off that Radio, it rots the scene,
  Besets our souls that Television Screen!

Overflow

The plenitude of spirit overflows,
The martial eagle stoops from out the blue,
The fattened steer amidst the fastness lows,
Slowly the sun mounts up to zenith true;
Soon beeves go gather to the random glade
And clump together in the silvan cool,
Grasshoppers cling, like halcyon arrayed,
To golden nectar-cups nigh lily-pool;
Wallow my dogs in water while I sit
Watching the mighty wheeling of a pair
Of secretary-birds which well befit
The Spirit of the Lord who writes on air:
I AM wide-wing'd and wild and wondous free,
This day thy Queen conceived God's word by Me.

For a Peal of Eight

An eastern isle of untold charm
Was once bombarded from the sea
With such an occidental psalm
That it was much upset like thee
Being informed that Yahweh's Three
Persons are Thought and Word and Voice
Of One Sole Substance which is Free
Love who is Chooser, Chosen, Choice.

Begetting Love is Father calm,
Begotten Love His Son is He
And Love Proceeding like a psalm
Is Charmer of St Peter's See
Who haunts it with His Melody
Singing The Thought, The Word, The Voice
Of which all knowledge has one She
Love who is Chooser, Chosen, Choice.

For a peal of eight times more alarm
Than Queen of Sheba had stands She
Who is the Queen of grace and charm
And Carmel, and of Persons Three
The Daughter, Mother and most free
Mistress that ever was in voice
Tuned to turn the atoneing Key
Love who is Chooser, Chosen, Choice.

Envoi

Prince, saunter up and down with me
And bid the cruiser's crew rejoice
Upon arriving at the Quay:
Love who is Chooser, Chosen, Choice.

Michael Ffinch 1934-1999

A Christmas Cantata

Shepherds keeping on the hillside,
Nursed the problems of the valleys:
Heard the angel-shouting echo
From the rivers and the gullies;
Saw the night-sky threaten wide
With the gaping of a calling;
Felt the midnight meadows falling
From the trances now denied.
Tracking from their hills in glory,
Where the glacier's ancient bow
Drew the worship of the valleys.
Took up stations in the story;
Wrapped their shoulders round in sheep
Gazed a baby out of sleep.

The Annunciation (from **Voices Round a Star** *– A Meditation for Christmas)*

She must have felt an inkling in the past:
Familiar winnowing of angel wings.
Alive, beside the almond leaves, a vast
Importance blesses like the words it brings.

Between the fearing and the unafraid
The tides of will are still and frozen:
No latitude to shout, to run, evade
The complex of the carefully chosen.

There were no afterthoughts she might forget;
No skilful metaphors through which to grope;
Its words were firm and gentle like a net.

Unchanged, she sat encompassed by their scope
And triumphed in the trap that Love had set
Beyond her adoration and her hope.

There was no interchange of doubt and trust.
Resolved, she passed her father's flocks and herds
And free, along the hill-track's fretful dust
She set to wrest her silence into words.

She watched as flawless eagles swooped to feed
And prayed for her who, anxious, counted days;
Who, like herself, would let her heart stampede
Across the open languages of praise.

Beyond the grassless crags, her mind engraved
A well-fed city starving for a guest;
Like bees among the orange trees, there craved

The doleful murmurs of the dispossessed.
She saw. The village white with sun, she waved.
A million voices mantled her and blessed.

Who could have seen in her delicate danger
The Hand beyond time surrender in light?
With Seraphim stride, one step to the manger,
A golden cave in a garden of night?

O who in his hour could tell her tomorrow?
A childhood of joy – a joy to obey!
Could linger the smiles that settle in sorrow;
Or measure from dark, her marvellous way?

Tell her out, Angels! Accomplish her Powers!
Spill, like a secret, her separate hours!
A girl for the blue! O Wonder-of-Wings!

Complete to her feet our fallen devotion,
Controller of Stars! O Star of the Ocean,
The sea of the confident cast-away stings!

Walsingham

Island of pity,
island of grace,
England has much in the mirror to face:
when Mary came to Walsingham,
this was a holy place.
When Mary came to Walsingham
she made an island blest.
made the Norfolk sky her own
that a heart might never hide alone,
a heart might find its rest.
For Mary came to show us home,
shelter of love and faith,
while in a trance
Richeldis knelt
and in her widowed longing
felt the calm of Nazareth.
By prayer and priest
the English east
became the beautiful,
the peaced,
the Little-House,
house of the poor,
where Mary liked to wait at the door
to see her children in.

Kings came,
ploughmen came,
pilgrims from Flanders and France;
turned with the tide
into Bishop's Lynn,
where river and quay,
as the ships veered in
rang with the Virgin's chants.
From wooded wold,
the fens,
and plain

the Chapel of St Catherine
harboured the hungry and the lame;
and candle-led,
before his shame,
from Barsham Manor
Henry came
beside his rightful queen.
But men had eyes on Walsingham,
misers in want and wealth,
who for politics and power
would desecrate our Lady's Dower,
our sanity and health.
Those wreckers came to Walsingham,
one silent August day,
seeing the Little-House was sound,
they swiftly razed it to the ground
and Mary's image then they found
and rode with it away.
They burnt her image
for the crowd
in London,
where the hate was loud;
on Thames-side
Thomas Cromwell stood
and put to flames the precious wood
to pacify the proud.
'Weep, weep, O Walsingham
whose days are nights.
Blessing turned to blasphemies,
holy deeds to despites.
Sin is where Our Lady sat,
Heaven is turned to Hell,
Satan sits where Our Lord did stay.
Walsingham, oh farewell.'

Coda

Will we go to Walsingham,
Will we give our time?
Will we draw on Mary's love
In youth, old age, or prime?
And will we bring ourselves away
From *Panorama* or the play?
Must all we be, when weekends come,
Blind pilgrims at the Stadium!

In Mary's land,
In England,
We'll shelter no denial,
But seek our home
In Walsingham,
Along the Holy Mile.

Maria

All that is gentle,
all that is strong
I need of you, my joy, Maria.
Gladden my grieving,
give me my song
safe from your hand,
Maria.
'This time is our time',
I hear you say;
all the paths in your garden lead one way,
your child in the centre
where you stand,
Maria.
Trust in my sorrow,
follow my flight
fast to your heart, my love, Maria.
Hasten your twelve stars
on my night,

your moon to my feet.
May England own you,
a garden again,
a rose in the hedgerow
after rain,
your child laughing with you
when we meet,
Maria.

Roger McGough 1937-

Defying Gravity

Gravity is one of the oldest tricks in the book.
Let go of the book and it abseils to the ground
As if, at the centre of the earth, spins a giant yo-yo
To which everything is attached by an invisible string.

Tear out a page of the book and make an aeroplane.
Launch it. For an instant it seems that you have fashioned
A shape that can outwit air, that has slipped the knot.
But no. The earth turns, the winch tightens, it is wound in.

One of my closest friends is, at the time of writing,
Attempting to defy gravity, and will surely succeed.
Eighteen months ago he was playing rugby,
Now, seven stones lighter, his wife carries him aw-

Kwardly from room to room. Arranges him gently
Upon the sofa for the visitors. 'How are things?'
Asks one, not wanting to know. Pause. 'Not too bad.'
(Open brackets. Condition inoperable. Close brackets.)

Soon now, the man that I love (not the armful of bones)
Will defy gravity. Freeing himself from the tackle
He will side-step the opposition and streak down the wing
Towards a dimension as yet unimagined.

Back where the strings are attached there will be a service
And homage paid to the giant yo-yo. A box of left-overs
Will be lowered into a space on loan from the clay.
Then, weighted down, the living will walk wearily away.

Seamus Heaney 1939-

Cana Revisited

No round-shouldered pitchers here, no stewards
To supervise consumption or supplies
And water locked behind the taps implies
No expectation of miraculous words.

But in the bone-hooped womb, rising like yeast,
Virtue intact is waiting to be shown,
The consecration wondrous (being their own)
As when the water reddened at the feast.

St Francis and the Birds

When Francis preached love to the birds
They listened, fluttered, throttled up
Into the blue like a flock of words

Released for fun from his holy lips.
Then wheeled back, whirred about his head,
Pirouetted on brothers' capes,

Danced on the wing, for sheer joy played.
And sang, like images took flight.
Which was the best poem Francis made,

His argument true, his tone light.

ENVOI

Henry Adams 1838-1918

Prayer to the Virgin of Chartres

> *Gracious Lady* –
> Simple as when I asked your aid before;
> Humble as when I prayed for grace in vain
> Seven hundred years ago; weak, weary, sore
> In heart and hope, I ask your help again.
>
> You, who remember all, remember me;
> An English scholar of a Norman name,
> I was a thousand who then crossed the sea
> To wrangle in the Paris schools for fame.
>
> When your Byzantine portal was still young
> I prayed there with my master Abailard;
> When Ave Maris Stella was first sung,
> I helped to sing it here with St Bernard.
>
> When Blanche set up your gorgeous Rose of France
> I stood among the servants of the Queen;
> And when St Louis made his penitence,
> I followed barefoot where the King had been.
>
> For centuries I brought you all my cares,
> And vexed you with the murmurs of a child;
> You heard the tedious burden of my prayers;
> You could not grant them, but at least you smiled.
>
> If then I left you, it was not my crime,
> Or if a crime, it was not mine alone.
> All children wander with the truant Time.
> Pardon me too! You pardoned once your Son!
>
> For He said to you: 'Wist ye not that I
> Must be about my Father's business?' So,

Seeking His Father he pursued his way
Straight to the Cross toward which we all must go.

So I too wandered off among the host
That racked the earth to find the Father's clue.
I did not find the Father, but I lost
What now I value more, the Mother —YOU!

I thought the fault was yours that foiled my search;
I turned and broke your image on its throne,
Cast down my idol, and resumed my march
To claim the Father's empire for my own.

Crossing the hostile sea, our greedy band
Saw rising hills and forests in the blue;
Our Father's kingdom in the promised land!
We seized it, and dethroned the Father too.

And now we are the Father, with our brood,
Ruling the Infinite, not Three but One;
We made our world and saw that it was good;
Ourselves we worship, and we have no Son.

Yet we have gods, for even our strong nerve
Falters before the energy we own.
Which shall be master? Which of us shall serve?
Which wears the fetters? Which shall bear the crown?

Brave though we be, we dread to face the Sphinx,
Or answer the old riddle she still asks.
Strong as we are, our reckless courage shrinks
To look beyond the piece-work of our tasks.

But when we must, we pray, as in the past
Before the Cross on which your Son was nailed.
Listen, dear lady! You shall hear the last
Of the strange prayers Humanity has wailed:

Prayer to the Dynamo

Mysterious Power! Gentle Friend!
Despotic Master! Tireless Force!
You and We are near the End,
Either You or We must bend
To bear the martyrs' Cross.

We know ourselves, what we can bear
As men; our strength and weakness too;
Down to the fraction of a hair;
And know that we, with all our care
And knowledge, know not you.

You come in silence, Primal Force,
We know not whence, or when, or why;
You stay a moment in your course
To play; and, lo! you leap across
To Alpha Centauri!

We know not whether you are kind,
Or cruel in your fiercer mood;
But be you Matter, be you Mind,
We think we know that you are blind,
And we alone are good.

We know that prayer is thrown away,
For you are only force and light:
A shifting current; night and day;
We know this well, and yet we pray,
For prayer is infinite,

Like you! Within the finite sphere
That bounds the impotence of thought,
We search an outlet everywhere
But only find that we are here
And that you are — are not!

What are we then? The lords of space?
The master-mind whose tasks you do?
Jockey who rides you in the race?
Or are we atoms whirled apace,
Shaped and controlled by you?

Still silence! Still no end in sight!
No sound in answer to our cry!
Then, by the God we now hold tight,
Though we destroy soul, life and light,
Answer you shall — or die!

We are no beggars! What care we
For hopes or terrors, love or hate?
What for the universe? We see
Only our certain destiny
And the last word of Fate.

Seize, then, the Atom! Rack his joints!
Tear out of him his secret spring!
Grind him to nothing! — Though he points
To us, and his life-blood anoints

Me — the dead Atom-King!
....

A curious prayer, dear lady! Is it not?
Strangely unlike the prayers I prayed to you!
Stranger because you find me at this spot,
Here, at your feet, asking your help anew.

Strangest of all, that I have ceased to strive,
Ceased even to care what new coin fate shall strike.
In truth it does not matter. Fate will give
Some answer; and all answers are alike.

So, while we slowly rack and torture death
And wait for what the final void will show,

Waiting I feel the energy of faith
Not in the future science, but in you!

The man who solves the Infinite, and needs
The force of solar systems for his play,
Will not need me, nor greatly care what deeds
Made me illustrious in the dawn of day.

He will send me, dethroned, to claim my rights,
Fossil survival of an age of stone,
Among the cave-men and the troglodytes
Who carved the mammoth on the mammoth's bone.

He will forget my thought, my acts, my fame,
As we forget the shadows of the dusk,
Or catalogue the echo of a name
As we the scratches on the mammoth's tusk.

But when, like me, he too has trod the track
Which leads him up to power above control,
He too will have no choice but wander back
And sink in helpless hopelessness of soul,

Before your majesty of grace and love,
The purity, the beauty and the faith;
The depth of tenderness beneath; above,
The glory of the life and of the death.

When your Byzantine portal still was young,
I came here with my master Abailard;
When Ave Maris Stella was first sung,
I joined to sing it here with St Bernard.

When Blanche set up your glorious Rose of France,
In scholar's robes I waited on the Queen;
When good St Louis did his penitence,
My prayer was deep like his: my faith as keen.

What loftier prize seven hundred years shall bring,
What deadlier struggles for a larger air,
What immortality our strength shall wring
From Time and Space, we may – or may not – care;

But years, or ages, or eternity,
Will find me still in thought before your throne,
Pondering the mystery of Maternity,
Soul within Soul – Mother and Child in One!

Help me to see! Not with my mimic sight –
With yours! Which carried radiance, like the sun,
Giving the rays you saw with – light in light –
Tying all suns and stars and worlds in one.

Help me to know! Not with my mocking art –
With you, who knew yourself unbound by laws;
Gave God your strength, your life, your sight, your heart,
And took from him the thought that Is – the Cause.

Help me to feel! Not with my insect sense –
With yours that felt all life alive in you;
Infinite heart beating at your expense;
Infinite passion breathing the breath you drew!

Help me to bear! Not my own baby load,
But yours; who bore the failure of the light,
The strength, the knowledge and the thought of God –
The futile folly of the Infinite!

BIOGRAPHIES OF PRINCIPAL POETS

St Bede (Venerable Bede) c670-735

Known as the 'Father of English History' for producing *The Ecclesiastical History of the English People*. In 682 joined the new monastery of Jarrow in Northumbria where he stayed for the rest of his life. Ordained priest in 703. Wrote numerous devotional works and translations into Anglo-Saxon. Canonised 1899; feast day 25 May.

Richard Rolle c1290-1349

Born in Yorkshire, and studied briefly at Oxford, but left aged nineteen to pursue the spiritual life. After some years of wandering became a hermit at Hampole near Doncaster, where he became spiritual director to a small nunnery. Had numerous mystical visions.

William Langland c1330-1395

Langland lived his life in obscurity, but some details are given in his great poem *Piers Plowman*. He was born about 1330 at Cleobury in Shropshire, and hoped to become a priest. However, lack of funds meant that he only took minor orders, forcing him to scratch a living by singing offices for the dead. He lived in London's Cornhill for some time with his wife Kit and daughter Colette. *Piers Plowman* was immensely popular during Langland's lifetime, and was written in three distinct editions: A around 1370, B around 1378, and C around 1392.

Geoffrey Chaucer c1343-1400

Chaucer was the son of a wealthy wine-merchant, and carried out senior diplomatic and commercial services for King Edward III. *The Canterbury Tales*, written in his retirement from public life in the 1390s, established him as the first great poet in English – 'the Father of English Poetry'. He was largely responsible for the adoption by English poetry of metre based upon regular stressed feet, replacing the older alliterative verse form.

Fr John Audelay c1360-1430

Virtually nothing is known about John Audelay, except that he was a priest of Hagmond Abbey. In his manuscripts he describes himself as 'blind, sick and deaf'.

Fr John Lydgate c1370-1451

For most of his life Lydgate lived as monk in the Benedictine monastery of Bury St Edmunds. A disciple of Chaucer, he was one of the most prolific poets of the late Middle Ages, though his work is now little regarded.

Fr John Skelton 1460-1529

Skelton was born in Norfolk around 1460, and studied at both Oxford and Cambridge. He became a priest in 1498, and was appointed Rector of Diss, Norfolk, in 1502. A man of great learning, he was described as the 'Light of English Literature' by Erasmus, and was tutor to the young Henry VIII. From 1511 he was overshadowed by scandal regarding an alleged concubine, and left Diss to rejoin his former pupil at court. He was censured by Cardinal Wolsey, who became a bitter enemy. Much of his verse is written in a distinctive, terse, almost breathless satirical form.

William Dunbar c1460-1513?

Dunbar was born in East Lothian, Scotland, and attended St Andrews University from 1475-1479. He became a Franciscan novice, but left the order before completing his vows to join the service of King James IV. He may have died in the Scottish military defeat at Flodden in 1513. Dunbar was one of the leading poets of the fifteenth century, and a pioneer of Scots as a literary tongue. (I have translated the poems given here into standard English.)

St Thomas More 1478-1535, martyr

A native Londoner, he studied law at Oxford, and then spent four years in a Carthusian monastery to test his vocation. More then left to pursue a legal career with great success. He was one of the leading scholars of his day; a friend of Erasmus, he became famous through his book *Utopia*. Through the 1520s he advanced in the King's legal service, and was appointed Lord Chancellor in 1529. He resigned in 1532, refusing to assist in the King's divorce. In 1534 More was arrested for refusing to recognise Henry VIII as head of the Church in England, and a year later was beheaded for treason on 22 June. Canonised in 1935.

St Philip Howard 1557-1595, martyr

Howard was the son of the fourth Duke of Norfolk, and Earl of Arundel in his own right. Brought up a Protestant, he converted to Catholicism in 1584, being greatly influenced by the bearing and arguments of Edmund Campion in his trial in 1581. He was imprisoned in the Tower of London for attacking the Queen's policy towards Catholics, and died there on 4 May 1595. Canonised 1970.

St Henry Walpole 1558-1595, martyr

Walpole was born in Norfolk of a Catholic family, and became a Jesuit in 1584. He was greatly influenced by the example of Edmund Campion, whom he praised in a long poem soon after the latter's execution, which Walpole witnessed, in 1581. Ordained priest in 1588, and with Fr Persons the founder of seminaries for the English mission. Landed in England in December 1593, but was immediately arrested, and sent to the Tower. Submitted to torture fourteen times by Topcliffe. Much of his verse was written in captivity. It should be read in the light of the fact that his hands were so broken by torture that he could barely write. He was executed in York on 17 April 1595, and canonised in 1970. Walpole was of a much gentler and more nervous disposition than Campion or Southwell, but like them stoically endured repeated, savage torture on the way to martyrdom.

St Robert Southwell SJ 1561-1595, martyr

Southwell was born of a gentle family in Horsham, Norfolk. He studied at Douai and Rome, entered the Society of Jesus in 1578, and was ordained priest in 1584. Aged only twenty five he entered England on a secret missionary expedition to persecuted Catholics. After six years 'on the run' he was arrested by priest-hunter Topcliffe in 1592. He was imprisoned for three years in the Tower of London, where he was tortured thirteen times. On 21 February 1595 he was martyred at Tyburn. Beatified 1929. Much of his poetry was written during the three years he spent in the Tower, and illustrates his deep faith. His poems were first published in book form as *St Peter's Complaint* in 1595, and were highly popular, running into many editions. Southwell's depth of imagery and powerful versification make him one of the most profound of the Elizabethan poets after Shakespeare, and one of the greatest religious poets in English. Canonised in 1970 as one of the 'Forty English Martyrs'.

Henry Constable 1562-1613

Constable was born of a gentle Yorkshire family, and educated at Cambridge. Describing himself as 'a Catholic and an honest man', Constable felt obliged to leave England, and spent most of his life in exile in France and Italy. On his return in 1603 he was arrested and imprisoned in the Tower of London.

William Shakespeare 1564-1616

William Shakespeare was born into a strongly Catholic family in Stratford-upon-Avon. His mother, Mary Arden, came from one of the prominent Catholic families of the area. His father, John Shakespeare, was one of the leading burghers of the town, becoming mayor of Stratford in 1568. He stood down from official duties after 1576, partly due to money problems, but probably due to reluctance to enforce increasingly stringent anti-Catholic laws. In 1592 John Shakespeare was himself charged with recusancy (failure to attend Church of England services), and his will (discovered in 1757) shows him to have been a committed Catholic all his life. As a young man, William Shakespeare is said to have left Stratford after a dispute with the local Protestant magnate, and taken refuge as a tutor in Catholic Houghton Hall in Lancashire. While there is no record of Shakespeare being prosecuted for recusancy, there is also no sign that he attended Anglican services. His first biographer with local knowledge, the Anglican Richard Davies concluded: 'He died a Papist'.

Ben Jonson 1572-1637

Posthumous son of a Puritan minister, and brought up by a bricklayer, Jonson was lucky enough to have a sponsor who paid for his education at Westminster School. He served as a soldier in the Low Countries in the 1590s, before coming to London as a playwright in 1597. He became a Catholic in 1598 while in prison for killing an actor in a duel, but returned to the Church of England in 1610.

William Habington 1605-1654

Habington came from an old Catholic family, and was educated at St Omer. His life was spent in quiet obscurity at his country house of Hindlip Hall, Worcester (a noted recusant haunt of the 1580s and 1590s). Habington seems to have taken no part in the Civil War. His courtship of his future wife, Lucy Herbert, is celebrated in his book of poems, *Castara*.

Richard Crashaw 1612-1649

Crashaw came from notable Puritan stock, but grew up as a High Anglican. He became a Fellow of Peterhouse College Cambridge in 1635, but in 1643 was expelled by the Parliamentary forces for his religious views. He went to Paris, where he was received into the Catholic Church in 1644. He became a minor canon at the cathedral of Loretto, where he died. His poems were published under the title of *Steps to the Temple* in 1646. He is generally regarded as one of the English 'Metaphysical' poets, along with Donne, Herbert and Vaughan.

John Dryden 1631-1700

Dryden was born at Aldwinkle, Northamptonshire, of Puritan ancestry. Educated at Westminster and Cambridge, he pursued the career of a man of letters, being appointed Poet Laureate in 1668. Initially known as a dramatist and satirist, Dryden showed deep religious and philosophical yearnings in *Religio Laici* in 1682. In 1685 he was received into the Catholic Church, setting out the reasons in *The Hind and the Panther* of 1687. He was deprived of his offices and official pension because of his Catholicism after the 'Glorious Revolution' of 1688 which overthrew the Catholic King James II.

Alexander Pope 1688-1744

Pope was born in London of a Catholic family, at a time when the Test Act of 1688 barred Catholics from university. Pope was of dwarfish stature and a cripple, and in constant pain from a curvature of the spine and asthma. A highly irritable man, he was also a good and generous friend, and the first man in England to make a comfortable fortune from writing. (After 1714 he was offered a government pension if he would join the Church of England, which he refused.) Anti-Catholic riots forced him to leave London for Twickenham in 1715, where he lived for the rest of his life. He brought the poetic couplet to a point of perfection, and his poetic genius was probably best expressed in satirical form such as the *Dunciad* of 1742.

John Henry, Cardinal Newman 1801-1890

Born and educated in London of a Calvinist family, he studied at Oxford and became a fellow of Oriel College in 1822. Ordained as an Anglican clergyman in 1824, he won great acclaim for his work as Rector of St Mary's Oxford. One of the major figures behind the Tractarian Movement, which aimed to reform the Church of England by studying its early Christian roots. In 1845 his studies convinced him to join the Roman Catholic Church, and he was ordained priest in 1847. He founded Oratories in London and Birmingham, and in 1879 was made a cardinal. Newman was one of the great writers of English; his spiritual autobiography, *Apologia Pro Vita Sua,* has become a classic, as have his many writings upon spiritual and educational themes. He wrote many hymns, and probably his best known poem is *The Dream of Gerontius,* later set to music by Elgar.

R.S. (Robert Stephen) Hawker 1803-1875

Born in Plymouth, Devon, and educated at Oxford, where he won the Newdigate Prize for Poetry. For many years Hawker was the Anglican Vicar of Morwenstow in Cornwall, where he restored a derelict church, built a school and established poor relief. A noted poet and Cornish antiquary. Received into the Catholic Church on his deathbed.

Aubrey de Vere 1814-1902

De Vere was born in Limerick, Ireland, and studied at Trinity College, Oxford. He was received into the Catholic Church in 1857, and thereafter wrote poetry mainly on religious and historical themes.

Fr Frederick Faber 1814-1863

Born in Yorkshire, Faber was educated at Harrow and Balliol College, Oxford. A close disciple of Newman, he followed him into the Catholic Church in 1845, and became a founder member of Newman's Oratory of St Philip Neri at Maryvale. Ordained priest in 1847, he moved to London where he wrote devotional works in conditions of great poverty. He is probably best remembered today for his hymns and translations of mediæval poetry.

Coventry Patmore 1823-1896

Patmore came from a prosperous family, and was privately educated. His father's sudden bankruptcy in 1846 forced him to go to work in the British Museum, where he stayed for the next twenty years. His marriage in 1847 made him blissfully happy, a fact commemorated in the series of poems on married love, *The Angel in the House* (1858). Distraught at his wife Emily's death in 1862, he travelled to Rome, where he was received into the Catholic Church in 1864. His poetic reflections on spiritual matters were published as *The Unknown Eros* (1877). In later life he was a friend and guide to Hopkins, Francis Thompson and Alice Meynell.

Dante Gabriel Rossetti 1828-1882

Son of Gabrielle Rossetti, first Professor of Italian at the new University of London, and brother of Christina Rossetti. He studied art at the Royal Academy School, and was a founder member of the artistic Pre-Raphaelite Brotherhood. His wife, the model Elizabeth Siddal, died in 1860, and he buried his poems with her. Notorious for exhuming her coffin in 1870 to retrieve his poetic manuscripts, subsequently published in book form under the title of *Ballads and Sonnets* in 1881. On his deathbed he called for a priest in order to be received into the Catholic Church, but died before the priest could arrive.

Christina Rossetti 1830-1894

Daughter of Gabrielle Rossetti, and younger sister of Dante Gabriel Rossetti. Her father's intense anti-clericalism inhibited her religious practice, but once he collapsed with a nervous breakdown Christina and her mother became devout Anglo-Catholics. Achieved fame with the publication of her first book of poems *Goblin Market* in 1862. Although an invalid for much of her life, she devoted herself to charitable work and the writing of mainly religious poems. The latter are generally of a high technical quality, and contain a strong element of renunciation and service.

Henry Adams 1838-1918

A descendent of two US presidents, Henry Adams was one of the leading historians and conservative thinkers in the US in the latter half of the nineteenth century. His poem, 'Prayer to the Virgin of Chartres', was unpublished during his lifetime and found among his papers after his death.

Fr Gerard Manley Hopkins SJ 1844-1889

Hopkins was born in Stratford, Essex, of a High Anglican family, and attended Highgate School and Balliol College, Oxford. He was received into the Catholic Church in 1866 by Newman himself, and two years later became a Jesuit novice. He was active in parish work in Liverpool and elsewhere until 1884, when he was appointed Professor of Classics at University College, Dublin. There he felt himself an outcast and a failure in this position, and his last years were marked with spiritual anguish. His highly original and innovative poems baffled most of his contemporaries, in particular his use of 'sprung rhythm', and few of them were published in his lifetime. After his death his manuscripts passed to his friend, the poet Robert Bridges, who did not publish them in book form until 1918.

Fr John Bannister Tabb 1845-1909

Descendant of an aristocratic family in the *ante-bellum* South, the Virginian Tabb fought for the Confederate forces in the American Civil War. After two years in a Union prison-of-war camp, he joined the Episcopal seminary at Alexandria, Virginia, but influenced by Newman he became a Catholic in 1872 and was ordained priest in 1884. Tabb taught English Literature at St Charles College, Ellicott City, Maryland, until his death. He would spend great time and effort polishing his succinct poems to make the reader think anew about the subject matter they conveyed; the poems themselves were not published in book form until after his death.

Alice Meynell 1847-1922

Born Alice Thompson, her childhood was spent travelling with her family in Europe. Suffered a spiritual crisis around twenty, resolved by her conversion to Catholicism in 1868. Married Wilfred Meynell in 1877. A noted poet and essayist in her own right, she helped her husband to edit the magazine *Merry England* for fourteen years despite having eight children. Her first book of poems, *Preludes*, was published in 1875, and six more volumes of poetry were published in her lifetime. Mrs Meynell was also a distinguished essayist. In 1895 she was seriously considered as a candidate for Poet Laureate, but her sex and religion went against her. (The nonentity Alfred Austin was appointed instead.) Alice Meynell knew most of the writers of the time, and was friends with Coventry Patmore and George Meredith. Her literary salon helped and encouraged younger writers such as Francis Thompson, Joyce Kilmer and Katherine Tynan Hinkson.

Digby Mackworth Dolben 1848-1867

Digby Dolben was educated at Eton, and decided to become a Roman Catholic despite the intense opposition of his father. He was a Benedictine novice but had not completed his conversion when he died in a swimming accident.

Francis Thompson 1859-1907

Thompson was born in Preston, Lancashire, the son of a doctor. He desired to become a priest, but his father forced him to study medicine in Manchester. Hating his medical studies, he repeatedly failed the examinations, and after six years' frustration had a nervous breakdown. Fled to London without qualifying. Attempts to live by writing ended in failure, and he was soon reduced to selling matches, and utterly destitute. For several years in the mid-1880s he lived the life of a tramp, sleeping rough on the Embankment near Charing Cross. Thompson dulled his misery with opium and alcohol. In 1887 Thompson was rescued from near-death by the Meynells, to whom he had sent some poems. They paid for him to go to hospital, although his health never properly recovered, and thereafter a long period of recuperation at Storrington monastery in Sussex, where some of his best poems were written. The publication of a volume of poems in 1893 established his literary reputation, in particular 'The Hound of Heaven'.

Louise Imogen Guiney 1861-1920

A New Englander, and daughter of a general in the Union army. For many years she was a senior librarian in Boston Library. She moved permanently to England in 1901. The author of essays and books on recusant history, as well as volumes of poetry originally published in the 1880s and 1890s.

Katherine Tynan Hinkson 1861-1931

A friend of Alice Meynell and Yeats, she was one of the leaders of the Irish Literary Revival of the 1890s. Born near Dublin and educated at a Dominican convent at Drogheda. Published volumes of poetry from 1885 onwards, and was a contributor to *Poems and Ballads of Your Ireland* (1888).

Fr John Gray 1866-1934

A handsome youth, Gray was a close friend of Oscar Wilde and the inspiration for Wilde's *The Portrait of Dorian Gray*. In 1890 he rejected Wilde's aesthetic philosophy and became a Catholic, and was ordained priest in 1901. He spent the remainder of his life as a parish priest in Edinburgh.

Lionel Johnson 1867-1902

Born in Broadstairs, Kent, Johnson was educated at Winchester College, and New College, Oxford. Editor of the Rhymer's Club 1892-94, and was regarded as one of the best poets and critics of the period. He broke with the decadents on his reception into the Catholic Church in 1891, and thereafter his poetry was mainly religious. Died in an accident.

Ernest Dowson 1867-1900

Dowson was the son of a London dry-dock owner, and received an irregular education. At Queen's College, Oxford, became a friend of Lionel Johnson, and later a member of the Rhymer's Club of young poets. Turned against the aesthetic movement in 1891, and became a Catholic. Died of tuberculosis, aggravated by drug addiction.

Hilaire Belloc 1870-1953

The combative Belloc was born in Paris while it was under siege by the Prussian army in 1870. The family moved to England, where he was educated at the Oratory School, Birmingham under Newman, and at Oxford. Bitterly disappointed not to be offered an Oxford fellowship, he came to London where he henceforth earned his living by writing. Became a British citizen in 1902, and was a Liberal MP from 1906-1910. An aggressive Catholic apologist, he was also the prolific author of historical, and political works. He is best known, however, for his children's nonsense verse, and as a polished essayist.

Mgr Robert Hugh Benson 1871-1914

Benson was the son of Edward Benson, later Archbishop of Canterbury. Educated at Eton, and Trinity College, Cambridge, he studied divinity and served as an Anglican curate. In 1903 he was received into the Catholic Church and was ordained priest in 1904. In 1911 Benson was appointed Private Chamberlain to Pope Pius X. He was a prolific author of religious works, poetry and historical novels.

G.K. Chesterton 1874-1936

Great friend of Hilaire Belloc, although a much gentler character. Born in London and educated at St Paul's School. He started to study art at the Slade School of Art, but a spiritual crisis caused him to withdraw, and he eventually entered publishing. A brilliant essayist, he spent most of his life as a freelance journalist. A prolific author, he is best known for his *Father Brown* detective stories, and literary criticism. Also wrote a number of works of popular theology such as *Orthodoxy*, *St Francis* and *The Everlasting Man*. Received into the Catholic Church in 1922, and thereafter a noted Catholic apologist. In the 1920s Chesterton campaigned for a more just economic society as head of the Distributist League.

Padraic Colum 1881-1972

Colum was born in Longford, Ireland, and educated at Trinity College, Dublin. After Yeats one of the major figures in the Irish literary revival of the turn of the century. Colum published several volumes of verse, the first being *Wild Earth* in 1907, and in 1911 he founded the literary journal, the *Irish Review*. He emigrated permanently to the USA in 1914, and was attached to Columbia University for many years.

Joyce Kilmer 1886-1918

Born in New Brunswick, New Jersey, and educated at Columbia University. Worked as a journalist, writer and editor. Received into the Catholic Church in November 1913 together with his wife Aline. For the next three years they both played a major role in the development of Catholic writing in the United States. In 1916 America entered the War against Germany, and Kilmer volunteered immediately. He was killed in battle in the summer of 1918.

Joseph Mary Plunkett 1887-1916

Son of a papal count, Plunkett was born in Ireland, but spent much of his youth wandering around Europe with his father. In 1911 he published a collection of poems, *The Circle and The Sword*. From 1913 to 1914 he edited the *Irish Review*, pushing it in a more political direction until it was suspended for advocating Irish independence in 1914. In 1913 Plunkett joined the Irish Republican Brotherhood, and was a leading figure in the Easter Rising of 1916. He was badly wounded in Dublin street-fighting, and was executed by the British on 4 May 1916, as was fellow poet Thomas MacDonagh.

Wilfred Rowland Childe 1890-1952

Born in Wakefield, Yorkshire, and educated at Harrow and Magdalen College, Oxford. He was received into the Catholic Church in 1914. From 1922 to 1945 he was lecturer in English Literature at Leeds University.

David Jones 1895-1974

Artist and poet, Jones grew up in Kent, and was wounded on the Western Front in 1916. His experiences of war traumatised him for the rest of his life. Converted to Catholicism in 1921, and lived and worked with Eric Gill on the latter's artistic community in Sussex for much of the 1920s. His long poetic work *The Anathemata* (1952), praised by Auden, was an attempt to revive the cultural impoverishment of modern life by returning to its Christian and mediæval roots.

Sr Maris Stella SSJ (Alice Gustava Smith) 1899-

Alice Smith grew up in Iowa in a Catholic family and was educated at the College of St Catherine, St Paul, Minnesota. In 1920 she was received into the Sisters of St Joseph. She studied English at St Catherine's, and went on to do an MA in Oxford. She returned to St Catherine's as head of the department of English, and was a prolific poet.

Caryll Houselander 1901-1954

Caryll Houselander was born into a Protestant family, but was received into the Catholic Church at the age of six, hence the title of her autobiography, *A Rocking Horse Catholic*. Her mother's erratic and travelling lifestyle meant that she had little formal higher education. Houselander was a mystic who received a vision of the Tsar's murder on 17 July 1917 as a symbol of Christ the King. A gifted poet and artist, she pioneered the use of art therapy to successfully help shell-shocked soldiers during World War II, and later worked with disturbed children. Writings included: *The War is the Passion* (1940), which described the spiritual basis of the war against Hitler; *The Reed of God* (1943) on Our Lady; and *The Flowering Tree* (1945), a collection of poems.

Roy Campbell 1901-1957

Roy Campbell was born in Durban, South Africa. A vigorous extravert – the complete opposite of the popular image of the thin, spindly poet. As a young man he sailed round the world on a schooner, raised horses and took part in bull-fights. He went to Spain in 1934, where he was received into the Catholic Church and fought on the Nationalist side during the Spanish Civil War. He volunteered for the British army during World War II, and served in North Africa. Campbell's deep love of Spain and the Spanish language underlie his profound translations of St John of the Cross. Died in a car crash in Portugal.

Fr John Lynch 1904-

Lynch was born in Oswego, New York, and studied at the Seminary of Our Lady in Niagara before being ordained priest on 25 May 1929. He spent most of his life as a parish priest in Syracuse, upstate New York.

Patrick Kavanagh 1905-1967

Kavanagh was born in Innislee, County Monaghan, to a traditional Catholic family. The son of a smallholder, he left school at twelve to go and work on the family farm. His best known work is probably *The Great Hunger* (1942), a verse epic telling the story of the terrible potato famine in Ireland in the 1840s.

John Bradburne 1921-1979

John Bradburne was born in England and served with distinction with the British forces in Asia during World War II. After the war he went through a period of spiritual searching, resulting in his reception into the Catholic Church at Buckfast Abbey. Attempts at a conventional monastic vocation failed, and he became a wandering hermit. From 1962 he was a helper at Mutemwa Leprosy Settlement in Zimbabwe. In 1979 Bradbourne was murdered during Zimbabwe's independence struggle. A mystic, and a Third-Order Franciscan, his poetry expresses his incarnational vision. The Church in Zimbabwe has started preliminary investigations into his beatification, driven by mass pilgrimages to Mutemwa.

Michael Ffinch 1934-1999

Ffinch was born in Kent, and educated at Repton and St Edmund Hall, Oxford, where he read English. He was received into the Catholic Church in his late twenties, and the Church remained thereafter a major force in his art and life. For most of his life he earned a living as a schoolmaster, while pursuing a literary career. His nativity poem, 'Voices Round a Star', was praised by Auden, the poem being later broadcast by the BBC in 1973. In 1972 Ffinch collaborated with the composer Francis Shaw to write the children's opera *The Selfish Giant*, which won first prize in an international competition. He was an admirer of G.K. Chesterton, whom he resembled in possessing the rare combination of bohemian behaviour and moral rectitude. Ffinch produced an admired biography of Chesterton in 1986, followed by a biography of Cardinal Newman in 1991. Ffinch's poetry covered a wide range, but his religious poetry was centred upon Our Lady and the joy of Christmas. He was also a distinguished nature poet, describing his beloved Lake District, and wrote a number of prose portraits of the area.

Roger McGough 1937-

Roger McGough was born in Liverpool, and educated locally and at the University of Hull. He burst into prominence in the 1960 with his poems for both adults and children. He was awarded the OBE in 1997, and this was followed by the Cholmondeley Award for Poetry in 1999. Roger McGough now lives in London. His *Selected poems 1967-1987* has been published in two volumes: *Blazing Fruit* and *You at the Back*.

Seamus Heaney 1939-

Seamus Heaney was born in County Derry, Northern Ireland, and he was educated at Queen's University, Belfast, where he later worked as a lecturer. He became a full-time writer after a spell as a lecturer at the university of Berkeley, California, and also moved south to live in Dublin. Heaney's first book, *Death of a Naturalist* in 1966, established him as one of the major poets of his generation, many of the poems exploring his agricultural childhood. His work continued to develop through the publication of such books as: *North* (1975); *Field Work* (1979), and *Station Island* (1984). In 1995 he was awarded the Nobel Prize for Literature. Heaney's own selection of his poems was published in 1998 as: *Opened Ground, Poems 1966-1996.*

Index of first lines